Vaster Than Sky
Greater Than Space

Also by Mooji

The Mala of God
White Fire
Before I Am
Writing on Water
Breath of the Absolute

Vaster Than Sky
Greater Than Space

what you are before you became

MOOJI

SOUNDS TRUE
BOULDER, COLORADO

Sounds True
Boulder, CO 80306

Published 2016

Illustrations by Mooji
Edited by Abe Gutmann, Joelle Hann, Sumantra Paul, Zenji Ganz,
and Gayatri Mascarenhas

Cover design by Jennifer Miles
Cover photo by Anna Kartseva (Amrita), © Mooji Media Ltd.
Book design by Beth Skelley

Printed in Canada

Library of Congress Cataloging-in-Publication Data
Names: Mooji, 1954- author.
Title: Vaster than sky, greater than space / By Mooji.
Description: Boulder, CO : Sounds True, 2016. |
   Includes bibliographical references.
Identifiers: LCCN 2016018603 (print) | LCCN 2016038639 (ebook) |
   ISBN 9781622037889 | ISBN 9781622037896 (ebook)
Subjects: LCSH: Spiritual life.
Classification: LCC BL624 .M66233 2016 (print) | LCC BL624 (ebook) |
   DDC 204—dc23
LC record available at https://lccn.loc.gov/2016018603

10 9 8 7 6 5 4 3

Dedicated to
seekers of Truth everywhere
for the benefit of all
beings

Contents

Introduction . . . xi

PREFACE   The Greatness of Being . . . xix

PART I   STEPPING INTO ONENESS

1   Is What You See All There Is? . . . 3
The Power of Self-Inquiry . . . 6
Freeing Up Your Being . . . 9
Self-Inquiry Guidance—Stay as the 'I Am' . . . 17
Self-Inquiry Guidance—
You Are Nothing Perceivable . . . 20

2   The Heart's Way to Truth . . . 25
The Call from Your Inner Being . . . 27
Devotion and Self-Knowledge:
Two Wings of One Bird . . . 29
Beyond the Psychological Mind . . . 37
The Heart's Way to Truth . . . 39

3   Transcending Our Conditioning . . . 45
Transcending Cultural Conditioning . . . 46
Moving Beyond Religious Tribalism . . . 50

Breaking the Spell of Personhood . . . 54

Merge with the Infinite . . . 58

4 The Person's Work Is Never Done . . . 63

The Theater of Consciousness . . . 66

Belief Must Become Reality . . . 68

Self-Inquiry Guidance—
Identity Implies I-Entity . . . 73

Dissolving the Mind's Residue . . . 76

Trust in Life . . . 80

Self-Inquiry Guidance—Remain Empty . . . 86

5 Go All the Way . . . 91

Beyond Opening and Closing . . . 95

Freedom Is Free—But Not Cheap . . . 102

The Ultimate Truth Is Not an Experience . . . 106

6 Grace Is on Your Side . . . 111

Backlash of the Ego . . . 117

The Guidance of a Master . . . 122

Bursting from the Cocoon . . . 127

PART II LIFE IN ITS DYNAMIC EXPRESSION

Your Life Is a Discovery . . . 135

7 Be in the World, But Not of It . . . 141

When You Want Truth *and* Worldly Success . . . 142

Your Place in the World . . . 146

Nothing Is a Distraction . . . 151

Self-Inquiry Guidance—Follow Me Inside . . . 154

8 Truth-Centered Relationships . . . 165

Let Love Be Rooted in Presence . . . 166

Relating Beyond Neediness . . . 175

Self-Inquiry Guidance—Facing the Suffering 'I' . . . 178

When Relationships End . . . 184

Wrap Yourself Around the Eternal . . . 188

9 Truth and Family . . . 193

Make Some Time to Discover the Timeless . . . 194

Your Life Has to Feel Right for You . . . 197

When Life Gives You a Shove . . . 202

10 Healing Through Transcendence . . . 211

Self-Inquiry Guidance—Stay as Awareness . . . 213

The End of Suffering . . . 214

When the World Seems Full of Cruelty . . . 223

11 The Self Alone Is Real . . . 235

Waking Up from the Waking State . . . 236

Beyond the 'I Am' Presence . . . 238

Just Sitting . . . 241

Glossary . . . 247

Acknowledgments . . . 251

About Mooji . . . 253

Further Information . . . 255

Introduction

VASTER THAN SKY, GREATER THAN SPACE arose from the inspiration to share Mooji's wisdom with those who are searching for lasting happiness, peace, and love—for Truth or what is often called Self-realization—but who may not be so familiar with self-inquiry or the nondual approach of *Advaita*. This way of looking into the truth of our existence is simple, direct, and powerful. However, it can appear complex and intimidating at first, because self-inquiry challenges our core beliefs and concepts regarding who we think we are and how we perceive the world we live in. Mooji often shares the story of when he first came across self-inquiry as taught by the Indian sage Sri Ramana Maharshi (1879–1950), who is credited with the revival of this ancient spiritual wisdom.

"After a powerful experience with a Christian mystic in 1987, my life underwent many changes, inwardly and outwardly, which culminated with my giving up teaching art at the local college. One day I was drawn to enter a spiritual bookshop in central London. I was not accustomed to reading books, but I was instantly attracted to a picture of Sri Ramana Maharshi on the cover of one book. His face radiated a warmth and light that immediately touched my heart. However, when I

opened the book, my reaction was, *Whoa! What is this?!*
His words felt very intellectual and noisy to me—so
much so that I actually thought the printer must have
made a mistake and put the wrong cover on the book.
The picture emanated such profound serenity, silence,
and peace, but the concise instructions of self-inquiry
within couldn't enter my being back then.

So I closed Sri Ramana's book and put it aside.
Instead, I found another book in the same shop
entitled *The Gospel of Sri Ramakrishna*, which
spoke to me immediately. Although I grew up in a
Christian tradition, the wisdom of the Hindu saint
Sri Ramakrishna was so universal that it touched and
conquered my heart. His every word resonated deeply
inside my being and was perfectly timed, as I had been
waiting to find a voice that would confirm the profound
experiences I had been having at the time. What I
learned later was that Sri Ramakrishna was not only a
great devotee—a *bhakti* saint—but also a completely
liberated sage from the perspective and experience of the
nondual *jnana* path—the path of pure self-knowledge.

In 1993, the urge and possibility arose for me to
go to India. I thought the sole aim and purpose of my
being in India was to visit Dakshineswar, the place near
Kolkata where Sri Ramakrishna had lived and taught. I
didn't know anything else. I had no *Lonely Planet* guide
or anything of the sort. And I was quite spiritually naive
back then—I knew nothing of gurus, spiritual paths,
or meditation, and certainly nothing of Advaita. I only
knew the divine love of Christ and Sri Ramakrishna.

Well, to this day, I still haven't made it to Kolkata. Instead, destiny's path brought me to meet my master, Sri H. W. L. Poonja, lovingly known as Papaji. And only through the grace and presence of Papaji, who is a direct disciple of Sri Ramana Maharshi, was I somehow able to read and to understand Sri Ramana's teachings inside my heart.

What I came quickly to see and understand was that self-inquiry is the most direct approach to Truth. And it *had* to be direct, because I have a very short attention span and am only attracted to what is straightforward, immediate, and simple."

In the years that followed, people began to gather around Mooji. Some would simply approach and ask if they could sit with him for a while because they felt so peaceful in his presence. Others began to ask him questions related to their own search for Truth. The capacity to guide them arose spontaneously, and what began as small informal gatherings quickly grew into meetings, or *satsangs*, with hundreds of beings.

In early 2012, Mooji was sharing satsang in Tiruvannamalai, in southern India, with around 500 people. Among them was Abe Gutmann, an American from Colorado who was immediately inspired by Mooji's capacity to guide beings into the discovery of their true nature with such unsparing clarity, wisdom, and humor. Over the next four years, Abe shepherded *Vaster Than Sky, Greater Than Space* into life by selecting, transcribing, and editing the most potent transcripts of satsangs he attended both in person and online. During satsang, Abe frequently asked questions regarding relationships, psychology, and our place in the world, because he felt that the answers to such questions would be well received by those new to satsang. This book came into being through Abe's dedication and persistence, which saw him restructuring the manuscript in response to feedback from Mooji and the Mooji Media Publications team.

In the summer of 2015, Mooji suggested that it was time for *Vaster Than Sky, Greater Than Space* to be finalized and released. With great synchronicity, as is ever present with a master, within days Abe received word that Sounds True was interested in publishing the book. The manuscript then underwent further revisions and refining by the Sounds True and Mooji Media teams, in consultation with Abe. This was a truly international coming together, with lengthy Skype editing sessions in early 2016 spanning Rishikesh (India), Monte Sahaja (Portugal), and New York City (USA). This process unfolded with grace and harmony during the five weeks of satsang with Mooji in Rishikesh, where more than 2,000 people attended—a beautiful reflection of Mooji's spirit and grace.

The book you are holding is the outcome of this collaboration. May it prove to be an invaluable guide to Self-realization through the unsparing light and wisdom of self-inquiry.

This is not a book to be read with the mind
The teachings and insights of Mooji are sublimely simple, and the place they lead us is beyond words. You don't need to learn any special techniques or practices, for self-inquiry is like looking into a mirror and recognizing your timeless face. However, as Mooji's own story shows, this introspection may at first be challenging, because it requires us to swiftly acclimatize to the language, potency, and immediacy of the pointings to the true Self.

Mooji uses language fluidly and metaphorically as clues to guide you into an inner, direct, and intuitive experience of the Truth you already are, yet are presently unaware of. As you read, don't get stuck on the precise meaning of individual words, sentences, or paragraphs. Instead, allow the energy of the words to enter your heart and being, without interference from the evaluating and interpreting mind, and you will find that, at some point, understanding just occurs naturally.

The main pointings are deliberately repeated in different ways throughout the book to offer space for this understanding to grow and ripen. The essential pointing to our true nature is simple and possible for everyone, including children, to grasp. However, it can take some time to empty and free our minds from the concepts we cherish about who we consider ourselves to be.

Although Mooji addresses many topics in this book, he actually only ever speaks about the discovery of our true nature. He often stresses that when seeking Truth, it is not important to know too many things. Therefore, the emphasis is placed not so much on teaching or learning, but on discovery and direct experience. If you encounter something that is not immediately clear or something that doesn't seem to make sense, don't be troubled about it. Let it be for now and remain open.

More important, when you do find something that resonates deeply, take some time just to be with that fully. Allow it to do its work internally. Mooji's encouragement to everyone is that one pointing, deeply understood and assimilated inside the heart, is enough to take you home.

Vaster Than Sky, Greater Than Space is rich in Mooji's wisdom and insights and is replete with the openness, love, and sense of humor that Mooji exudes. It also contains many of Mooji's favorite teaching stories and clear self-inquiry guidance. It is structured in such a way as to guide those new to Mooji and his teachings into the direct recognition and experience of Truth. For those already familiar with these pointings, it offers the great opportunity to deepen into final understanding.

Part I, Stepping into Oneness, introduces Mooji's core teachings and insights. Chapter 1, in particular, conveys the essence of self-inquiry; as such, it is a chapter to be revisited again and again until one thoroughly understands self-inquiry and is able to use its power to attain final liberation.

Part II, Life in Its Dynamic Expression, is based on questions concerning our place in the world, relationships, family, work, difficulties in life, and so forth. While such matters are not usually the focus for Mooji, he addresses these topics because they arise for many—in particular, for those who are new to this profoundly simple way of looking into our timeless nature. As he steadfastly points us back to our source Being, Mooji demonstrates that Truth is highly practical and not separate from life. In fact, Truth enriches every aspect of the manifestation and the experiencing thereof.

Vaster Than Sky, Greater Than Space was compiled from living dialogues that are arranged by subject to make it easier for new readers to follow. However, this book should not be taken as a comprehensive view of Mooji's responses on any of these subjects. As a living master, Mooji responds spontaneously to the call of the moment, and as is the case with true masters, his approach may at times seem to be inconsistent and even contradictory. Remember here that he answers not only the question but also the questioner, as guided by his intuition.

The book is not overly structured in a way that would appeal to the logical, conditioned mind. Mooji knows and communicates with the deeper intelligence innate in every human being, and so, he credits each and every one with the capacity to awaken through recognition. He knows the value of learning, growing, and expanding when challenged to discover the all-encompassing Being we are.

"Very often in our culture, you are treated as though
you have little spiritual capacity, as though you have no
inherent power, and that people 'in the know' have to
always liquidize your food in order for you to grow. But
it is important that the true seeker understands that they
must be open enough to be deeply challenged to awaken
the living aspiration necessary for true freedom. To be
free you are going to have to break out of the mold
of personal conditioning, out of your cocoon. Each
sincere seeker must be willing to undergo the necessary
transformation from caterpillar consciousness to the
butterfly of freedom!"

The Greatness of Being

I WOULD LIKE to remind you of the greatness of Being, that all we ever need is to be found in the Self. All that we seek in this world that is truly lasting—true happiness, joy, peace, light, space—are inside of us. They are ever present, but for a while we don't see them because we search for fulfillment in the field of the ephemeral, the changeful. Only at the eleventh hour do we turn to the Self. Such procrastination is not wise, though it is common.

For thousands of years, human beings have been exploring the nature of who we are and the purpose of our being here on this planet. Many found what they were searching for, but billions of forms who were once called "people" are no longer here. They are gone. And now it is *our* turn—we are the living wave. We entered into manifestation to walk on this planet as contemporaries and to take our chance at finding that which is imperishable in us. All of us have this opportunity to find true freedom, and no one is exempt, no one is disqualified, because the light of consciousness burns in everyone.

The world encourages us to look from the limited sense of personhood—a very unstable standpoint from which we are always trying to find balance on very shaky ground. But you must learn to look from your source Being. Your Being is vaster than sky, greater than space—and it is already here. Look from your stillness, not from your agitation. You don't have to go even a fraction of an inch away from where you are right now to find the silence and stillness of your Being. And from here you can observe the energetic streams that are pulling your attention to go out into the field of noise and personhood, where beings are suffering from person-poison, from the toxicity of ego.

You have picked up this book, and some power within you has brought you to find something deeper than you have found so far. And it is so simple! Begin by looking from the place of your stillness: it is already here. Don't combine yourself with any mode of time or any concept, and immediately you will find yourself in a realm of neutrality, spaciousness, and silence. Even if the tree of the mind is shaking furiously, that movement is watched from the place of stillness.

Learn to cultivate this habit of paying more attention to the stable sense of Being rather than to the agitated sense of *becoming*, because the becomings are unending. Get acquainted with the stability of Being; get used to the feeling of emptiness. It will not harm you. In fact, by so honoring your Self, you will come into a field of great joy, peace, love, trustworthiness, and aliveness. This is true self-respect. You will lose nothing from the world of activity—it will go better because you will no longer be wasting energy, and misconceptions will fall away. It is win-win all the way. I wonder why it takes us so long? Are the fruits of the world so sweet that they could compete with the beauty of your own Self?

This is a mighty existence, and it is beyond our human capacities to comprehend its full potential. But in the simple steps that are being pointed to here—of reverting the attention back to the place of stillness and silence within—we may realize that potential.

It is time to leave behind childish attitudes and begin to pay a little more attention to what is really here. This is a time-body, a mortal body, but an immortal presence is moving in it. While the body is still warm, use this bodily life to rediscover your timeless Being.

Mooji

Stepping into Oneness

Truth is what we are.
It is our essential nature and Being.
It is the pure Self, the limitless One,
the ultimate reality—it is awareness itself.
But we have become unaware
of the magnificence of our true nature
on account of our upbringing,
conditioning, and education,
which paint a very different picture of who we are
—and all of which we believe.

Is What You See All There Is?

MANY YEARS AGO in my school days, a boy showed me a small picture, a very simple black-and-white image just a bit larger than a postcard. He asked me, "What do you see?" I thought he was joking because it was so clearly a white vase on a black background. I asked, "What is this, a trick question?"

But he insisted, "*Really* look at it. What do you see?"

"It's a white vase on a black background, plain and simple. No decoration, just the shape! Is there something more?"

"Yes, you are missing something because you are only looking in one way." By now he was getting impatient, so he said, "Can you see the two faces? Look from the white to the black."

Ah! Suddenly I could see that there were two identical faces looking at each other. Then he asked, "And the vase? Can you still see the vase?"

I hadn't bothered about trying to see the vase again because I was still so excited to be seeing the faces. "No, I can't see the vase! What happened to the vase?"

He tried to help me see, "Look at the picture. See the vase again!" I looked and looked, until again it was the vase. Then, all of a sudden, I could see both the vase and the faces simultaneously through just a slight shift of perspective and focus.

Obviously no change had occurred to the picture itself—the shift was only in my perception.

We all start out looking at life from the particular perspective of our upbringing, which provides us with assumptions about who we are. For most of us, this culturally imparted point of view simply remains our perspective as we move through life. There are seven billion people living on the face of the earth, but rare is that being who goes through life seeing more than the conditioned body-mind—only the vase—as who we essentially are. Very few question their belief in their identity or personality, and thus they miss the opportunity to realize their true nature.

Although the metaphor of the vase and the faces is a good illustration of how we perceive a limited reality based on our conditioning, it also falls short. The Truth that I am pointing to is beyond just being able to visualize from a new point of view and then from multiple perspectives. It is about discovering that there is a deeper reality to what we see and that reality is always here—we must simply come to recognize it as our very own Self.

Spirituality is the search for perfect understanding, for Self-discovery, for Truth, and it must take place right where you are. The Truth that you are searching for must already be right here, for it is timelessly present.

What is Truth? Truth can never be merely a holy cluster of concepts, conditioning, or beliefs. It is not an event, nor is it an object apart from you in some sacred vault. For Truth to be Truth, it must be unchanging, immutable, ever present—yet it is beyond characteristics and conditions. It cannot be anything that comes and goes, for everything changeful arises *from* it and comes and goes *in* it. Truth is what we are. It is our essential nature and Being. It is the pure Self, the limitless one, the ultimate reality—it is awareness itself. But we have become unaware of the magnificence of our true nature on account of our upbringing, conditioning, and education, all of which paint a very different picture of who we are—and all of which we believe.

If you open your inner eyes, you will see the Truth that lies right here inside of you beyond the transient play of phenomena we call life—beyond everything we can see or perceive. When I say *beyond*, I don't mean beyond in terms of distance, but beyond in terms of subtlety. The search for Truth is not about running away from the things of this world but about understanding their ephemeral nature. And more than that, it is about discovering our true nature as an inherent stillness from where even the subtlest movements of phenomena are being perceived.

Those who discover that reality of their inmost Being enjoy a sense of peace, love, and wisdom as its natural perfume. They experience their essential nature as true freedom. Here you are invited into the direct experience of that timeless reality through the method of self-inquiry, which forms the essence of this book.

Seeing from our true position, our true Self, we come to understand that the appearance of any phenomenon doesn't mean it is true or real in and of itself. To discover the Truth, we need to look for the one who *sees* all phenomena—can that ultimate seer itself be seen?

What capacity, what power is present here inside of us that we are able to contemplate and inquire into our ultimate nature with such subtlety. This type of looking into the truth of our nature and Being is also called satsang, which means association with the highest Truth. Satsang comes in innumerable forms—sitting in the physical presence of a master, following the guidance offered in a book such as this, working in the garden, playing with your children. Once you have the eyes to see it, every movement of life itself is satsang, calling you home to your limitless Being.

Welcome to satsang.

The Power of Self-Inquiry

In the traditional way of learning, during childhood we start simple in our knowledge; as we grow older, we become more complex. Now, as we search for Truth and turn the spotlight toward ourselves, we encounter much complexity initially, though we are in the process of evolving back into simplicity.

Some people say that realizing the Self is difficult. I am here to show you that, on the contrary, it is exquisitely natural and effortless. One might rightfully ask, "If self-inquiry is so direct, why don't more people seem to discover the truth of who they are?" As I often say, Truth is simple, but the seeker of Truth is complex. We have been missing the obvious because we have been giving too much importance to what rises and falls inside our Being. This is like seeing only the waves while missing the ocean itself.

Truth *is* here, so let us take a look at what conceals it. This is the power of self-inquiry. What was hidden is quickly exposed. What is genuine is revealed. It is so immediate in its impact that all that is unreal is brought up to the surface quickly: we see what we are attached to, whether or not there is resistance to change, and we uncover the hideouts and cul-de-sacs of false identity.

Everything is presented in the here-and-now. In the energy field of satsang, what might have taken seven to ten years to process is being compressed into two or three days. We get straight to the point. What need is there to advocate strenuous practices of such lengths of time when Truth is ever present as our very own Self? All that is required is that we recognize our real position as the ultimate witness—formless and immutable.

When I say that these pointings to the Truth are direct, I am not saying that satsang is like a shop where you come to buy enlightenment over the counter then go away all nice and shiny. Rather, even within presence, and even in the midst of the joy and freedom of Self-realization, a soft alertness or vigilance to the varying schemes of the psychological mind continues. And so, if something were to arise that seems to veil our true nature, it is easily detected. If there is any avoidance, cleverness, or pretense, it will swiftly be rooted out. You will know what is real and permanent and be able to distinguish that timeless nature from what is transient.

Some people are tired of practice, but *practice* should not be considered a dirty word. Self-inquiry is also a practice of sorts. Especially in the beginning, it requires steady determination, commitment, and a sense of responsibility to your own Self. However, such practice is not felt as a burden but rather as a way to keep your witnessing fresh.

So Calm

Once it happened that people came on a silent retreat with me on a small island in Ireland. One afternoon, we observed a group of people taking a ride on the sea in a hovercraft. Because these crafts go very fast, skidding and bouncing hard on the surface of the ocean, the crew always straps you in tight. About eight or ten of us went for a ride. They had strapped us in carefully, and we had already enjoyed part of the ride sitting in silence. Then, while at full speed, everyone spontaneously started taking off their seatbelts to ride the waves standing up. The captain didn't even tell us to sit down and buckle up! When we came back to shore, we thanked him for the fantastic time.

The next day the captain showed up at satsang. I had just been telling everyone about the experience when I noticed him: "Ah, here is the captain himself!"

Then he said, "I came because I take many people out on the sea, but I never see people this calm. When they were out on the water, everybody was so still, yet they were enjoying the whole experience. That is why I was not at all concerned when everybody started to stand up. So I wanted to see what this was all about."

There is something profound about being in satsang in the heart. It is not merely something mental, not just a pile of information. Somehow your heart comes and takes over your mind. It is almost as if you live life with a tongue-less spirituality that speaks for you even if you don't speak about it. Something shines from that inner core. That's why they called the Buddha "The Radiant One." It shines when you are free of your mind, free of past, free of intention, free of desire, free of identity.

Freeing Up Your Being

If someone were to interview you every six months for thirty or forty years, you would notice that what you had to say about yourself was different at each stage of life. You might also recognize that at each stage you were always convinced that your views were those of a stable entity, saying things like, "This is just how I am! You can't change a leopard's spots!"

One time you may say, "I strongly believe that we should be doing such-and-such," and then several interviews later, "I strongly believe that we *shouldn't* be doing such-and-such; we should be doing that other thing." It's such a changeful picture. Which of these identities is the real you?

If I were to ask you what your thoughts were at exactly 7:44 a.m. this morning, would you be able to recall them? No. We can't even remember what we were thinking this morning, yet we tell stories from when we were fifteen years old and grant them great significance. We are often treading on the very shaky ground of memory, which can be highly distorted. But for the most part we remain unaware of this.

Even as we begin to examine our beliefs about ourselves more deeply and thus come to the moment where we recognize that they are false, we somehow remain convinced that we are the person we *think* we are at any given point in time. Despite recognizing the changeful and unstable nature of identity, we all too often continue to identify with the mind, which thrashes about in the time-bound realm, analyzing the past in an attempt to be better prepared for the future:

I said it this way, but I should have said it that way.
I knew I should not have done that—never again!
Why did I go? Why didn't I go?

Everything we want to accomplish takes time. But what is it that takes no time and requires no effort? What is it that is not in the region of time? No need for clocks. There is neither day nor night here. A great spaciousness opens up and a sense of peace pervades your being when you find that you are this timeless, unchanging, untouched awareness within which all experiences arise. You intuitively know that you are in the right place inside your true Self. You recognize that these bubbles of thought—or indeed any phenomena—are not your essential Being; rather, they are generated by and held inside this great harmony or one-ness that you are.

The Simplest Step

The step into oneness is the simplest step. You don't need a spiritual or religious background to take it. "Be in your natural state" is such a straightforward message that I can even share it with children. They respond well and are happy just to be in that feeling of being, not identifying with mental imagery or thoughts and without being located in time or confined to any particular shape. If you just stay like that, it eventually becomes effortless.

The state of presence—the sense 'I am' or 'I exist'—is natural for everyone. No one needed to teach you this. When this sense 'I am' combines itself or becomes associated with other states and ideas, it is as if those states become a part of what 'I am' is. But they are not original to who we are.

From a young age, we pick up many false assumptions about the world, about life, and about exactly who we are living life. The concept *I am the body* is the core belief we adopt very early on. Once we have accepted this basic *I am the body* concept as who we are, other concepts can now pour on top of it: *I am a man or a woman. I am ambitious. I am lazy. I am interesting. I am intuitive. I am like this or that.* And so a unique psychological identity forms.

Mostly we assume that this identity is an unquestionable fact, and yet those acquired beliefs are not part of our original nature. We take ourselves to be a particular body with a unique personality, and this perspective remains with us as we live our lives. Taking this person-identity to be true, we perceive ourselves as a separate entity in a world of many other separate entities and objects.

> ALL THAT WE REFER TO AS BEING OURS—OUR BODY, OUR MIND, OUR EMOTIONS—IS *NOT* WHAT WE ARE, ESSENTIALLY.

You could write many pages on all the nuances of your personality: *I am this particular type of person; these are my tendencies, my dreams, my aspirations, my possessions; this is my experience, and these are my certificates to prove it.* But all that we refer to as being ours—our body, our mind, our emotions—is not what we are, essentially.

If this is too much to take in at once, let's break it down.

Everything you can perceive comes and goes, including your own body. You are the one looking at time, objects, and even thoughts and emotions. Through the senses, you are able to observe everything that is perceived as life, as manifestation, as existence. And behind the eyes—in the realm of thought, emotion, and memory—these are perceived with the eyes of inner perception. Your sense of being a particular person is also perceived.

Regardless of whether the object of perception is physical and can thus be measured for color, shape, and size, or whether what is being perceived is something more subtle like thought, feeling, and sensation, *all* are phenomena. It is the sense of 'I' that perceives them. First 'I' must be there. One can say it is the password into this mighty game of existence. Only after 'I' comes 'you' and 'other'—world, friends, education, desire, religion, and so on.

So now the question must be asked: 'I' implies what? Who or what is 'I'?

When questions like these are asked, don't look for a verbal or mental answer, and don't trust so much in the mind and learned knowledge. Rather, look inward and see what these words point to. The nondual wisdom of Advaita invites you to find out for yourself what 'I' really is—whether it is what you assume or imagine it to be.

Most people have a strong sense of being individuals and hold the conviction that they determine their own experiences and are familiar with their own realities. That may be true to an extent, but it is only a lesser, relative truth. The greater Truth is that you *are* the awareness within which the idea of yourself living a life and *having* awareness is appearing.

In other words, the 'person' we take ourselves to be is an idea emerging in consciousness as an expression of consciousness. This idea has other ideas about itself—for example, *I am a body that has consciousness and an independent life to live.*

Here is a joke that illustrates this confusion well: A man sitting in the doctor's waiting room has a frog sticking out of the side of his head. When it's his turn, the nurse accompanies him into the doctor's office.

The doctor says to the man, "So, what's going on here?"

The frog replies, "Well, Doc, it started out last week as a small lump on my bottom, and it just kept on growing bigger and bigger!"

Aren't you surprised that the frog replied? So much in our lives is based on conditioned thinking that we insist on believing. What we have been brought up to believe is that we *have* consciousness. And I say no! At the level of the body-mind and the personality, we are the *product* and *expression* of consciousness.

But because of our cultural conditioning and inherited ways of thinking, all based upon the idea of *personhood*, this simple assertion I have just made—namely, that each of us, as a person, is the expression of consciousness rather than its creator or controller—seems illusory, evasive, and elusive. We insist that we just don't get it. We may even experience a kind of nausea because we are not used to thinking like this.

We are accustomed to a certain way of thinking, but there are ways of understanding that bypass the personal thinking mind and are profound in their impact. Mind in its natural, intuitive function is a higher power than the personal mind mode. The natural mind operates in a much broader way. It is not obsessed with activity or identity. It is clean and clear, empty and fresh, so life simply unfolds. One stays in complete harmony without strain or effort. The natural mind is in a state of grace.

When you are established in and as the Self, whatever is going to happen will just spontaneously arise out of that oneness. If you study and learn as a person, you can only function as a person—maybe as a good person, a skilled person—but when you awaken to the Truth, you start moving as a whole environment. When something arises that needs to be done, that need is recognized, and a movement to fulfill it begins, and other streams join in until it becomes a river. You see how the forces join together. Then you are actually looking at this whole matrix of life and seeing that it is the One doing it all. You're not merely thinking this—you are actually seeing it with God's eyes.

At this point, allow some space for understanding to happen without the interference of your logical mind. Your mind cannot take you there. Just be empty, without relating to any thought, intention, or identity. Like this, beyond mind's efforts, you stand a chance of discovering the naturalness of life and being.

We Only Think We Are the Body

Usually our experience of life is not, *I am consciousness!* Instead it is, *I am the body that has consciousness.* But let us take a moment to really look at this idea. It is not the body that says, *I'm aware of you.* The body hasn't said anything like that. The body makes various kinds of noises, but I don't think that it has written a book yet or made any grand statements. The body is innocent in all this. Rather, it is *you* who says, *I'm aware of the body.*

We are all living in time-bodies. From the birth of this body, each of us is like a candle that has been lit and is burning down throughout the course of our lives. And at some point, the flame of the body will go out. But *you* are not essentially the body, the senses, or the mind, because they all report to something that observes them.

Suppose you had parked your car outside and someone said, "There's a blue car with the lights left on." You would say, "Oh, that's *mine*," not, "That's *me*."

Similarly, we can say, "This is *my* body—it is not me because I am here to perceive it. I am looking at my hand. My hand is not looking at me." My hand—not me.

"My eyesight used to be so good that I could read a license plate from a hundred yards, but now I can't even see you." My sight—not me.

"I used to believe this and I used to believe that, but now I gave up those beliefs." My beliefs—not me.

"My memory used to be really sharp, but now I have trouble recalling what happened a few days ago." My memory—not me.

A relationship collapses: "My life is over; no wife, no life." My *life* is finished—not *me*.

So if you leave aside all these things that you say belong to you but are not *you*, everything else is seen as secondary to who you are. The true Self is primary.

What we are is consciousness. The body is the vehicle through which consciousness can taste experiencing. And in the human form, consciousness has the capacity and opportunity to realize its own source and thus come into a direct experience of this.

Currently there is a belief inside of you humming, *I am the body*. To discover our source Being, we must find out who or what that 'I' is. Is it really the body? The feeling *I am the body* is itself a thought. It might feel like a very deeply held conviction, but that doesn't make it real.

I'm not asking you to get beyond this identification with the body just like that. No, leave aside the thought that you *are* the body or you *are not* the body. Just come to the point of recognition that something is here that is aware of the body and of everything else that arises for you. That very awareness that the body and the senses seem to report to is also aware of objects, of the sense of distance, height, weight, of the sense of 'I' and 'otherness.' Everything is reporting to this essential inner perceiving principle, isn't it? But the awareness itself is not caught in the bubble of experiencing. It is your very own immeasurable Self.

Look, confirm, and be one with the awareness Self.

Following *I am the body* is the thought *I am the doer of actions.* This idea says to us, "If I am the doer of actions, then I'm responsible for the fruits of those actions. And I'm also going to be the one who suffers or enjoys the fruits of those actions." It seems obvious, in human conception, to accept this kind of logic. So we judge people based on the concept that they are the doers of actions and the thinkers of thoughts.

But those who have gone a bit more deeply into their own introspection have come to see that it's not quite true that we are independent entities so firmly in the driver's seat. The vital force, the animating power of the universe, is somehow moving in each body and activating even the movements of thoughts, sensations, and apparent decisions. All this is happening in the presence of the witnessing consciousness, which itself cannot be said to be a "happening."

Identification with the body is a state that consciousness needs to experience for a while. But eventually, grace will compel consciousness to transcend this severe limitation and guide it home to its original nature.

If you continue to look inward in this way you will start to see more clearly. Self-inquiry begins by looking to discover whether the personal identity, with all its conditioning and idiosyncrasies, is who we truly are. And it ends as a mirror in which the timeless is reflected.

Stay as the 'I Am'

We are all familiar with the sense of being. Without practicing anything, we spontaneously refer to ourselves as 'I.' Each person can confirm, *I am, I exist.*

Am means "to exist, to be." The sense of existence is naturally present and feels totally comfortable. It is the beginning of perception, and it functions during the waking state as the effortless witness and observer of all that arises. This feeling *I am, I exist* is the natural untaught way through which we recognize our existence.

But who is the 'I' that *am*, the 'I' that exists? Let's look together. The practice of self-inquiry is powerful enough to take you all the way from identification with the body to unshakable and lasting peace.

Start with the feeling *I exist.* It takes no time, for it is already naturally here before any thoughts arise. It is no distance from you, so you don't have to go to it.

Don't look for the 'I am'—you *are* the 'I am'! It is naturally here as consciousness. Just be self-aware.

Don't let this natural feeling of presence combine with any other concept, thought, or intention. All intentions such as *I want to accomplish such-and-such, I hope this inquiry pans out,* or *I want to become enlightened* should be left aside. Stay with the vibration of presence—not merely the words, but the intuitive, subjective sense of being—*I am, I am here.* That's all.

The mind may creep in and say, "Well, I don't *see* anything; this isn't working out," and then it will mischievously start playing the usual distracting person-noise to draw away your attention. But you just remain in the sense of being, *I exist*. If the attention starts to drift off, don't worry. Just bring the attention back to the simple 'I am.'

Practice this inquiry for short periods of about five to seven minutes at a time. You can do this with eyes open or closed, while seated or while walking—it doesn't matter. In the beginning, you may find it easier to just sit by yourself. Try to find a space and time when you are least likely to be disturbed, though this is not a condition or requirement. Remember: wherever you are, the sense of presence must be there. It is there without any effort at all. The fact that you can know you are alive and awake is because the sense 'I am' or presence is there first.

THE PRACTICE OF SELF-INQUIRY IS POWERFUL ENOUGH TO TAKE YOU ALL THE WAY FROM IDENTIFICATION WITH THE BODY TO UNSHAKABLE AND LASTING PEACE.

Just focus on what this exercise is aiming at. Stay with the natural sense 'I am,' the feeling of being. In the beginning you may feel tired, as though you are having to make a great effort to keep this sense 'I am' from mixing with other thoughts. Other thoughts come and want to play, but do not engage them. Just be with the 'I' feeling.

Gradually, with a little practice, you will see that the sense 'I am' stays by itself, without intrusion, and you will start feeling a sense of expansiveness and peace. A natural feeling of wanting to stay more in this state will develop, but just start out like this, with brief periods of five to seven minutes of self-observation. ❧

The Fruits of Self-Inquiry

If you follow through with the inquiry with full heart and mind, then strong identification with the body and societal conditioning will change radically. That is a change in the idea of who 'I' am. It is a shift in orientation from being the conditioning, from *I am this body, I am this person, I am the son of so-and-so, the mother of so-and-so*, to being the witness, the one who is without belief systems, the one who is synonymous with the very ability to observe. You will arrive at the realization that you are just joy itself, and everything you do arises out of this joy, out of this spaciousness, light, and love. As the sense of personhood thins away, you begin to experience life more panoramically. At first, life, as seen by the personal mind, may seem real; you take yourself to be an individual 'me' making decisions and living your life accordingly. Then, you may come to see it as a play that is somehow unfolding effortlessly. And at a certain point, you will see it's all just a kind of Is-ness.

These observations are not intended to mystify your mind, but to bring it into the complete simplicity of being. I may talk like this here, but when I'm moving about in my daily life, I'm not thinking about these things at all. I don't lie in bed at night thinking, *Oh, yes, you know, the pure consciousness and the mind.* But I am compelled to talk about it while it remains unclear to those in search of the living Truth.

We think it is so important to maintain a certain way of behaving and speaking. But I say, no, there is ample room in my Being for watching some TV, for enjoying some reggae and the occasional soft drink. Why not? How can I step out of my own Being? There is no need to be especially religious. I don't even have to be "spiritual." There is nothing I have to be or do. I don't even have to be myself. For me, this is freedom, even beyond the concept of freedom. I am the immutable Self.

How simple life is until belief and identity are poured into the mind. A whole realm of mind that is naturally quite magical is instead invested with plenty of energy with which to manifest a mundane and limited personal existence. But beyond the cultured mind are higher and more refined ways of seeing: the realm of awakened being.

I DON'T HAVE TO LIVE LIFE, NOR DO I "HAVE" A LIFE TO LIVE. I *AM* LIFE.

Here, everything enters into joy, light, and peace. I don't have to live life, nor do I "have" a life to live. I *am* life.

At a certain point, you will see that this body has never imposed any limitation upon what we are or upon what is. All of those limitations are only being dreamed. Everything—even apparent disharmony or difficulty—is this magnificent, magical consciousness. Everything is magical but also, somehow, seemingly ordinary. However, the liberated one dwells beyond this realm of duality as the untouched seer—unborn awareness.

SELF-INQUIRY GUIDANCE

You Are Nothing Perceivable

Anything that you perceive cannot be what you are.

Simply observe this internally until it becomes naturally confirmed in the mind. *You* are earlier than anything perceivable. Stay as the awareness of this. Observe that all thoughts and sensations, all phenomena, come and go in front of you.

Notice that you are already here before anything appears on that screen of consciousness. You perceive this effortlessly.

The computer is on but you don't log in. Simply look. You will feel an inner spaciousness opening up in the immensity of being. Let this be your exercise as you move about in daily life: keep your focus on the sense of being rather than on the appearances arising in the mind space.

Being in this state of presence will reveal inner strength and awareness. But you may find that your mind tries to escape from it. Just observe this tendency. In the beginning, the force of distractedness will feel difficult to resist because the attention has been accustomed to drifting toward mental activity and trivia.

As this tendency is noticed, greater understanding will emerge. By continuing with detached witnessing, the pull to escape will begin to weaken, and an increased sense of presence will be felt. You are at the very door of awakening. But be aware that the tendencies, habits, and deceitfulness of the psychological mind will not be so easily transcended.

It isn't that you have to suppress this energy of the mind. Rather, be in the witness state, with its natural, spacious, and omnipresent nature. It is your own true Self. Therefore, don't waste energy and time trying to control the mind. Just stay as the impersonal awareness.

As you watch, you will come to recognize that identity itself is just a thought, running from one story to another like a monkey jumping from branch to branch. In the past, it may have gone on for hours without you being able to catch it. But stay as awareness and you will find that your vibration is more open, loving, and free and that your consciousness is rising to a higher altitude. It will be much easier for you to catch the mind, because as soon as identity starts playing, an inner signal will light up, and you will quickly be able to recognize this play.

Now, this is very important: who or what is witnessing the playing out of this identity? Don't let the mind answer for you. Try to understand what is really being asked here. Don't be in a hurry; remain focused. Check in and verify the natural sense 'I am here.' As what are you here? You may respond, "I cannot say or see anything in particular. It's just a sense of being."

Keep returning to the *being* position. Develop the habit of observing from and as presence rather than as person. Through the state of presence, you will quickly grow in wisdom and intuitive insight. You will begin living in the high-altitude realm of presence, above the region of the psychological mind where the sense of personhood resides. Here the personal mind cannot breathe. It fades in its seeming power to influence the presence.

When the idea *I am the person* is sieved out, there remains just the 'I am' presence.

Allow time to marinate in this profound state of awareness-seeing-being. It is the *Satchitananda* state. *Sat* means existence, *chit* is consciousness, and *ananda* means pure joy or bliss. All beings love this divine state. The play of personhood emanated from it and is sustained by it for a while, until there arises sufficient maturity in personhood to merge back into presence. All this is the divine play—the *maya*, or play of God.

Beyond Presence

At the appropriate time, further maturing occurs to the presence. A realization may arise inside the being: the 'I am' is also seen, the 'I am' is also perceived. The sense of presence is also felt. A deeper space is intuitively felt, beyond presence; it is totally nonphenomenal. This maturing is also the action of grace and cannot be understood by the mind. Don't be in a hurry for this.

To come to the sense of just the unmixed presence is already tremendous. You are in the field of grace.

Remember, the presence 'I am' is the Godly principle. 'I am' is the Christ light, the Shiva being, the Krishna consciousness. It cannot be dispelled as mere illusion. It is the active God-Self, the dynamic expression of absolute awareness. Without it, there can be no experiencing, nor can there be the realization of the Self.

The Absolute is not revealed through human effort. At the appointed time, presence simply begins merging in it. If you try to force this, you will bring the mind and person in again. It will seem as though the mind has accomplished something tremendous, but it will be a fake realization, a mere mental state.

Apply yourself fully to the introspection offered here. It is good for all seekers. As you deepen in the inquiry, you naturally find that the inquiry is happening, that life is unfolding, but you are not charting your movements or measuring yourself against the phenomena arising as mind. Everything is fresh, and the attention no longer strays as before; it remains easily one with immutable Being.

This self-inquiry is your internal work. Internal work—eternal satisfaction. Internal work revealing timeless Self.

You have tried it the hard way . . .
now try it the heart's way,
the effortless way, for a while.

I have not come to burden you
but rather to free you of the notion
that you need to do anything to be your Self.

The Divine is not even an inch away from you.
It can never be apart from you.
It is the core of your very Being.

The Heart's Way to Truth

SOME PEOPLE ARE strongly drawn to spirituality, while others think that spiritual seekers are all weaklings. It is never easy to say exactly what causes one's attraction to the pure Self to emerge. In most cases, this attraction will not lead to a sudden flash of Self-discovery, but rather to a gradual maturing.

Papaji, my own master, used to tell a story that illustrates this point well.

The Fisherwomen and the Florist

Some fisherwomen were accustomed to walking through a forest to get to the sea. There they would wait for the fishermen to come back with the catch. Then the women would put all the fish into baskets and carry them back on their heads to the village to sell.

One day, three women had collected all the fish and were returning to the village through the forest, when suddenly the monsoon arrived with a *bang!* Lightning was flashing, rain was pouring down, and with the strong winds blowing, they were afraid of falling coconuts. On the way through the forest in this state of panic, they passed by a small house. It was the home of a florist, which also served as her flower shop. When the florist saw the fisherwomen running, she called out, "Come, come! Take shelter in my home!"

Quickly they ran to the florist's house. She said, "You simply cannot go on in this storm; it would be too dangerous! Please spend the night here. The fish will stay fresh outside in the wet air."

They gladly accepted the invitation and set down their fish baskets on the veranda. The florist showed them into a room that was full of flowers: lavender, jasmine, beautiful roses, and so on.

"Stay here tonight, you will be fine," she said.

Like this, they all lay down, but none of them could sleep. One of them was even very restless and kept fidgeting.

"What's wrong?" asked the eldest fisherwoman.

"I can't sleep; it smells horrible in here!" exclaimed the restless one.

"I can't sleep either, with the stink of these flowers in my nostrils!"

"What shall we do?"

So the elder one said, "I know what we can do!" She crept out onto the veranda, got one of the fish baskets, held it out in the rain, shook it a bit, and brought it inside. Now at last, all of them fell asleep and slept like babies, because they were accustomed to the smell of fish.

Fish gave these fisherwomen a comforting feeling. The fragrance of roses, jasmine, and lavender was horrible to them. They could not enjoy the flowers. And so it is with us. It is almost as though we have to reacquire the taste for our own higher nature. This is why most people, at most times in their lives, are on a kind of slow-cook setting. Being completely identified with their personality, they would find it unbearable if suddenly their identity were to be dissolved in pure consciousness.

The Call from Your Inner Being

Although the Truth is timelessly present, our seeming journey of realizing it has its place in the realm of time and change. When you become attracted to Truth, there may first be a season of exploring different paths until you find one that resonates deeply. When this happens, you may feel a natural sense of commitment. But it should not be the result of a pressured choice based on the concept that one *has* to make a choice in order to benefit from one's seeking. You just seem to be carried along in a bigger wave. Your heart, rather than your head, chooses.

If a choice is not arising for you, then enjoy the exploration. Maybe the result is that you will see the same thread moving through all these beads. When you have reached the top of the mountain—the height of your Being—you can see all the paths. Some are short and direct, others, long and meandering; all are an authentic expression of consciousness.

In 1987, I met Michael, a young man who I felt to be a saint. He was worshiping with a group, so I began to go to church with him. The members of his church were very dynamic and sincere young people. The catch was that I didn't like the preacher; I felt that he was very narrow-minded. At the time, the Muslims were making inroads into the previously Christian-oriented environment of the Jamaican community in London, and he preached that Muslims were the ones to beware of and to actively oppose. I didn't feel that any such pushback was necessary, and the preacher's railing against them bothered me. Because of this, I started to find myself less in the middle of the group, then on the edge of the group, then in the hallway, then by the front door. Finally I was out and never went back.

I started to move on my own, but it was all okay, because a profound impact had already taken place, and I had begun to speak to God directly. I experienced a most beautiful love affair with God that gave me the confidence to move forward, but little doubts would still pop up as to whether I had done the right thing in leaving the church. Occasionally I would meet someone from the group, and they would say, "What? Have you abandoned Christ?"

When they used this type of language, I would ask myself: "Have I done that?" Then I would look inward, and it was clear that, no, I hadn't abandoned Christ. In fact, he was (and still is) alive in my heart.

Even so, I underwent many struggles, and I had much to learn, but guidance always came to me from the inside. Looking back now, I can see that my life was an unfolding: my inner map only showed the way forward, not back. Everything that was needed to nurture me came to me.

So, I am supportive of people exploring until they are deeply touched by something. When it does happen, it will feel like a natural settling in. You may like Advaita *and* Buddhism, or you may be drawn to something else. That's fine. Don't force yourself into a commitment to any particular way.

Find the Buddha or Christ in you. Buddha was not a Buddhist, and Christ was not a Christian. Go to the source—you don't have far to go. You don't have to take even a single step, because it's all here right now. Find this Truth, and when you do, you may also find that you still enjoy and appreciate the various expressions of spirituality. You can enjoy them, but you will now be standing in the very heart of their unity.

So I say, turn inward. It is not religion that's calling you. Rather, the call is from your own inner Being. Your psychological identity may come forward with a little resistance, but if you persevere, you will discover the ultimate Truth of your Being—the source of true joy, peace, and freedom.

Devotion and Self-Knowledge: Two Wings of One Bird

A woman who was struggling with prayer came to me seeking advice. She told me that previously she had loved praying and had trusted completely in its power. But when she started to do self-inquiry, she began to feel that whenever she prayed, the sense of unity lessened and the sense of duality increased. She held a concept in her mind that in order to pray there must be two: the one who prays and God. But self-inquiry was revealing that there is only one consciousness playing as many. She began to reject prayer, thinking that it was keeping her bound in duality.

This is not an unusual projection when one looks with the mind. But from that place of pure Being, prayers and hymns to the Supreme are no different from nondual contemplation. Whatever concept we may have of God, the pure reality of God is beyond our concept. Even nonbelievers may find themselves praying to a higher power in times of desperation or need, for it is an instinct in human beings to acknowledge this power. Beyond 'I' and 'Thou' there is only One. But, still being caught in the mind's clutches, we are in no position to dismiss God. We are simply not yet ready or willing to merge into oneness.

If there is an urge within to discover the Truth, prayer may also arise spontaneously from a sense of intimacy or trust in the Supreme. So, you may find yourself saying, "All that I conceive myself to be I leave here at your feet. Absorb me in You." This is where inquiry and prayer meet, and such a request is so powerful that it cannot be denied. It may not make sense to the mind, but you will spontaneously come to understand and thus be transported into the presence of God. Ultimately, there are no dialogues in the world; it is all a divine monologue. For in reality there are not two; there is only the single reality in its appearance as many. One could say that if duality has any meaning, it is to venerate the Supreme, which, in the highest sense, is the Supreme in praise of itself.

If saying prayers is considered a practice, then it must be transformed into something quite innocent. When a child calls out to its mother, "Mommy! Mommy!" is the call considered a practice? Prayer is a plea. Its soul is the yearning behind the call. But sometimes people may not feel that prayer is an expression they can relate to. So, if you don't feel called to pray, I say, you don't have to. If the feeling to pray isn't present, but instead there is a strong pull toward self-inquiry, know that the grace and power to look inward also comes from God.

Don't Make Tattoos Out of Any Teaching

One may call self-inquiry a pathless path, and I have found it to be the most direct way to Truth. However, I'm not speaking against other spiritual paths, especially if they ultimately guide you home.

By treading a path with many practices, you may indeed arrive at your goal in time, but what often happens is that you end up journeying for a very long time. You may also be laboring under the weight of a whole backpack of beliefs and concepts, and that has its perils, because there are so many hidden thought processes and preconceived notions that can mislead the traveler into taking a wrong turn.

ULTIMATELY, THERE ARE NO DIALOGUES IN THE WORLD; IT IS ALL A DIVINE MONOLOGUE. THERE IS ONLY THE SINGLE REALITY IN ITS APPEARANCE AS MANY.

As spirituality came into my life, I initially felt that I was naturally of a more devotional, or bhakti, temperament. I was not of a mind to want to control or understand life, but rather to leave things in God's hands. It came very naturally to me to see and accept that all is God's work and to live in that mode of humility and surrender to God's will. My attitude has always been: "No need to test me, God, because You know that I am going to fail. All is You and Yours."

As I mentioned, in my hometown in England, I met a man of faith named Michael, and I was deeply touched by his presence. Now, I was originally brought up in Jamaica in a Christian culture. People were very comfortable with talking about God and faith. The Jamaican community in England, where I had lived since my teenage years, was no different. One would meet people from many denominations. They would talk religion, and many people were flexible and open. But others interpreted that openness to mean that you were "up for grabs," and so they would try to proselytize you into their denomination—or at least get you to buy into their take on spirituality and God. So I was accustomed to these kinds of discussions.

But this man Michael was different. In talking with him, you didn't get the feeling that he was trying to convert you to his belief system. Rather, there was something curious about his presence that made me wonder, *What is it about this man?* I felt warmed by his presence, and that warmth produced a spark that kindled an interest in the living faith that he embodied. Through asking him questions and finding that he embraced my curiosity and cooled my doubts, I was satisfied by him and by what he had to say.

Then, one day, he was visiting me. There were four of us, and we had a beautiful time together. When he was about to leave, I asked, "Michael, next time you pray, will you pray for me?" He said, "Yes, but why not *now*?"

So he prayed with me with his hand on my head, and when he was finished praying, I found myself praying to God. The supplication poured from my own mouth: "God, please help me! Help me!" It was a turning point in my life. Something took place in me and suddenly I felt so happy, so light, and so peaceful. I didn't want to go to bed that night. I thought that if I were to sleep, that beautiful feeling would fade.

But when I opened my eyes the next morning, it was still there. I had a little window in my room, and the sun was shining in as little rays of light. It was like I was seeing sunbeams for the very first time in my life; as if a dimmer switch of sensitivity had been turned up and the sense of beauty and harmony that had already been there was experienced at a much higher level. A deep peace had entered my being—and it has remained here ever since.

Subsequently my life began to change, and no one had to convince me about what I intuitively knew as Truth. I felt like I was seated in the lap of God. When that feeling came, it was clear: this feels right. I knew that I would offer up my entire existence to this. I didn't go through any mental contortions. Maybe that was because of my temperament—I wasn't a philosophical guy with a lot of sophisticated ideas. My feelings were very simple: either you liked something or you didn't. Maybe this lack of gray areas and perceived complexities was helpful for me because I wasn't always deliberating and asking myself, "Is this the highest state of consciousness?" I couldn't have answered that question at the time anyway. Words like *consciousness* or *the Absolute* were not even in my vocabulary yet.

In my early conversations with Michael, he was not trying to convince me of anything. It was all happening in a flow. We would speak, and his words were simple, like telling a story to a child.

I would say things like, "Sometimes this feeling comes." I don't even remember what I would ask him, but it would be of that kind of simplicity—nothing hugely philosophical or impressive.

Then he might answer, "I wouldn't bother with that. I would just leave it alone."

And I would say, "Okay, thank you." Straight in, with no need for elaboration. I just understood.

The rest was just a change in the manner that I was moving about in life. The ego would stick its neck up, but I didn't call it ego. I just knew it was the false bit—it was trouble.

At first, I thought I could pick and choose who to send blessings to. But it didn't work, and I would just make a mess of things. I felt so pained and humbled by what I perceived to be my failings, and the pain was much greater than what it would have been before. These lessons were very sharp and painful—as if God had slapped my hand. It was just that simple.

In this growth process, I didn't study any big books. I bought some books, but I really had no idea what to read. One book was about runes, and I simply didn't get what it was talking about. In another book, a priest and a philosopher were debating, and I thought, *What in God's name are they talking about?* Such discussions seemed strange to me. I was in the feeling, and the feeling was so alive, whereas the feeling and vibration of the words in the book seemed really heavy. I wondered who would want to follow such lines of philosophical speculation. *Did I have to follow it?* I was overwhelmed at the thought.

One day, in a spiritual bookstore in central London, I was attracted to a picture of Sri Ramana Maharshi on the cover of one book. His face radiated a warmth and light that immediately touched my heart. However, when I opened the book, my reaction was, *Whoa! What is this?!* His words felt very intellectual and noisy to me—so much so that I actually thought the printer must have made a mistake and put the wrong cover on the book. The picture emanated such profound serenity, silence, and peace, but the concise instructions of self-inquiry within couldn't enter my being back then.

So I closed Sri Ramana's book and put it aside. Instead, I found another book in the same shop entitled *The Gospel of Sri Ramakrishna*, which spoke to me immediately.

Although I grew up in a Christian tradition, the wisdom of the Hindu saint Sri Ramakrishna, a devotee of the fierce goddess Kali, was so universal that it touched and conquered my heart. I was quite spiritually naive back then—I knew nothing of gurus, spiritual paths, or meditation, and certainly nothing of self-inquiry or Advaita. Yet his every word resonated deeply inside my being in a sweet and magical way. It was perfectly timed, too, as I had been waiting to find a voice that would confirm the profound experiences I had been having at the time.

What I learned later was that Sri Ramakrishna was not only a great devotee—a bhakti saint—but also a completely liberated sage from the perspective and experience of the nondual jnana path—the path of pure self-knowledge.

This all happened by itself, and something in me just trusted in that process. Something touched my heart and penetrated deeply, and I knew it wasn't an everyday occurrence. It was strong, and I just walked in that vibration. How could one not walk in such a vibration! I was so full of overflowing peace. The feeling of love was like a subtle electric current passing through my body, but it was deeply peaceful. I didn't even want to sleep just to be in this feeling.

At some point the urge arose inside me to go to India. I had no money, but grace came in the form of my sister, who asked me to paint a mural of our hometown in Jamaica in her bathroom in London. She was disabled and couldn't get about. We had both grown up in a rainforest by the sea, and so I recreated this ambience, which was very uplifting for her. I had previously worked as a street portrait artist and as an art teacher in college, and I applied myself to this mural with great attention and devotion.

When I finished the painting, my sister gave me quite a bit of money, and I immediately bought a ticket to India. I thought the sole aim and purpose of my being in India was to visit Dakshineswar, the place near Kolkata where Sri Ramakrishna had lived and taught. However, instead of bringing me to Kolkata, destiny's path brought me to meet my master, Papaji, who is a direct disciple of Sri Ramana Maharshi. What I was then able to see and understand was that self-inquiry is the most direct approach to Truth. And it *had* to be direct, because I have a very short attention span and am only attracted to what is straightforward, immediate, and simple.

So people may ask, "If God is Supreme, and you met God in 1987, why wasn't that enough for you? Why was it necessary to come to India to meet Papaji, another human being, in order to approach the Truth through Advaita?" Maybe it is because in 1987, I wasn't yet ready to relate to the innermost reality. I knew that God was everywhere and in all things, but I wasn't yet ready to accept my oneness with this supreme power.

Whereas Michael had helped me open up to God and all of creation through devotion and prayer, starting in 1993 with Papaji, I learned how to recognize that self-same God in my own heart as well as in the world around me. Then for a while, I was only drawn to this nondual practice of self-inquiry. And what did that inquiry lead me to discover? I came to see that all are one: prayer, inquiry, God, and Self. Whether it's by means of true surrender or through authentic self-inquiry, the result is the same: freedom from the ego's influence and from the confines of the personal identity by waking up from the hypnosis of conditioning. Prayer and inquiry, devotion and self-knowledge, bhakti and jnana—they are like two wings of one bird, the bird of Freedom.

On the path of inquiry, you may know a deeply contemplative state that lays bare mischievous concepts and that has the power to break them open and zap them. Another time you may reject *everything*, even the very idea of yourself. At yet another moment, you may be praying to the Supreme, "Rid my mind of ego and merge me in You. Replace me with You." Then you might decide to recite mantras—but not because you have a checklist of practices to perform; rather, it just unfolds. All of this is you. It simply arises like this at one moment and like that the next. Many attitudes may present themselves along the path, so don't make a tattoo out of any teaching! You accept everything.

Beyond the Psychological Mind

We feel that the sense of ourselves as the doer of actions must be in place in order for things to get done. However, when we are quiet—meaning when we don't engage with thought activity and instead rest in the natural sense of being—we quickly discover that the vital force expresses by itself, and it does so spontaneously, without any intention whatsoever. If you truly give this a chance, you will experience the beauty and harmony of life when you are rooted in being rather than in doing.

Before, the mind may have had much more influence. If it said, "Come, let's go," you went. If it warned you, "Don't go," you stayed put. It was as if you were the mind's servant. But as you merge ever more into the unity-heart, the psychological mind's voice will become but a distant murmur.

Remember, by *mind* I am not referring to mind in its purely practical functioning. This will continue, and there is absolutely no trouble with that. The practical mind doesn't leave behind the bad smell of identification.

The *psychological* mind, on the other hand, is that aspect of consciousness that is identified with and caught up in the personal story. It reminisces about the past and projects into the future. It tries to control life and make it accord with the ideas it has of how things should be. It will offer up all sorts of suggestions, excuses, and distractions, but it derives life only from your attention, interest, and belief. It might even say that you're not good enough for Self-realization.

And maybe it has a point.

You—as the idea you have of yourself—*aren't* good enough! You must transcend the personal aspect of mind if you want to be free. Notice what the mind would suggest and, most important, notice to which 'I' the mind speaks. Who is the mind speaking to? Is it addressing the true Self?

For the woman who was struggling with prayer, what in her was capable of observing the lessening of the sense of unity and the increasing of the sense of duality when she prayed? What observes such fluctuations? What is its measure, and what yardstick can measure it? Looking in this way is the essence of self-inquiry.

Keep quiet and simply observe. You will find that it is *you*—but not you as an ego. The ego also has the capacity to witness, but it witnesses with self-interest. When this is seen, a deeper space opens up behind it and you are in your pure witnessing. This is you, the 'I am' consciousness that witnesses all phenomena, including ego and the increase in the sense of duality. You see that these are only movements and are momentary in duration. If you don't pay much heed, they won't even register as having happened.

Until and unless the mind says something is happening, experientially nothing is happening. When we impart power to the psychological mind by giving it importance, it intimidates us, and we suffer from its tyranny. It's like a nation selling weapons to its enemies. However, even this is only a seeming. It isn't true. *You* are the one who determines whether a particular phenomenon is powerful or not. The mind in its psychological portrayal cannot intimidate the pure Self; it can only intimidate the idea we have of who we are.

So, if you feel drawn to self-inquiry, leave aside your pet concepts and just inquire. If you feel drawn to prayer, then pray. But don't buy into the idea that the two approaches are mutually exclusive. Don't hold tightly onto any idea or utterance. Don't be a one-trick pony! Simply follow the guidance and experience the outcome. You don't have to say, "Okay, I believe in this or that method." The purpose is not to believe but to go to the space beyond belief into perfect understanding. However, if belief helps break down the superstructure of egoic identity, then it is serving its purpose. The wise keep their minds open until understanding comes to them naturally and unforced.

The Heart's Way to Truth

Any spiritual practice, or *sadhana*, should emerge from an authentic inner movement. It shouldn't come from a mental projection—a desire to get somewhere or to derive some particular personal benefit from it. Sadhana should not be done mechanically.

Some spiritual practices are time consuming and complex, while others like self-inquiry are direct and immediate, each to suit the temperament of the seeker. Some seekers enjoy the journey of spirituality but may secretly be afraid of reaching the destination, while others are tired of practicing and just want to discover Truth. The latter attitude—that of immediacy—is alive. I like it when people have the sense of urgency because that is when the miracle of existence can begin to reveal itself.

I am speaking directly here because I don't want to put anything between the seeker and what is sought. Wherever there is the space to point to Truth directly, I will take that opportunity. What we imagine to be obstructing our journey to Truth is not ultimately real, because we *are* the Truth. I know that it is not easy to grasp this, as we have a strong belief in our identity as a person seeking Truth. But there is nowhere you need to go to find Truth. Where are your efforts going? What are they trying to accomplish? The Truth is the very same as the one who perceives the effort being made.

When you grasp what I'm saying, you will see that all efforts are being expended just to try to find the one who is watching the efforts. All efforts that you make are watched in you. Awareness itself absorbs all exercises and practices.

While some practices may benefit the physical and energetic body, it is mainly the mind that likes performing exercises. It wants to be the one working on *vasanas*, moving through the *chakras*, doing breathing exercises, applying blue lights and crystals to cleanse the aura; it likes to be engaged and in charge, and such efforts make you feel you are *doing something* to attain Self-realization. But I tell you now, abandon the idea that you can practice your way into enlightenment—this idea is a trap and reinforces your sense of being a person.

Mostly, we are in a partnership with the mind instead of hiring it as our employee, and this allows it to veto anything we propose. I point you directly to awareness, but the mind wants to avoid awareness and to keep you asleep. Why? Because the mind will not give up its power. It seemingly lays claim to all it sees—that which is visible to the eye as well as what lies in the field of emotions and memories. But ultimately the mind has to admit: "I can devour anything phenomenal, but I cannot eat awareness, for it devours me."

The Effortless Way

Perhaps you have performed many practices and have derived some benefit from them, but now you have been drawn to this direct and simple way of self-inquiry. I'm not going to give you seventeen steps to anything. Not even a single step! Lay down your arms, lay down your techniques for a moment, and take some rest. Feel your heart again.

You have tried it the hard way. Now try it the heart's way, the effortless way, for a while. I have not come to burden you but rather to free you of the notion that you need to do anything to be your Self. The Divine is not even a fraction of an inch away from you. It can never be apart from you. It is the core of your very Being.

What would bring my heart the greatest joy would be if every single heart were to open and discover the Self. I don't see any real impediment to this awakening except for fear, stubbornness, or strong identification with one's own sense of autonomous personhood. These apparent obstacles are nothing new, so we must be familiar with their weak points by now. They can all be removed because none of them is greater than the Self. They may form themselves again from time to time, but you will make good use of challenges as mirrors with which to look at your own Self.

The simplicity of Being, the naturalness of the Self, requires no technique, strategy, plan, knowledge, or learning. Don't keep cultivating. Just keep quiet for a bit. I have found that living in this immediacy is to live on top of the world. But humanity has forgotten to trust that the wind of grace will fill its sails and has, instead, put so much energy into its own vain efforts.

Don't worry about things so much! When you stop worrying, your eyes become bright again; your heart open, clean, and pure; and you feel that your whole life is wind assisted. Grace accompanies you as you move; it carries you along the way. Indeed, grace is already there before you reach the place it has carried you.

The Divine is right here, right now, yet we seem to miss it. Although it should be obvious, habit seems to veil the Real. Follow this simple advice and come out of this jungle of the mind. Let's discover this Truth together. I am only reminding you of the simplicity of your Being that can never be polluted, never go wrong, and never be destroyed. It can never belong to the devil, and it can never die. You cannot damage it. You cannot improve it, because it is always perfect. Open up to its presence; it is not different from you. Grace brought you here, and grace is serving your awakening.

What I point to is *Brahman*, the Supreme Reality.

Brahman is like the sun, which just by being enables all life-forms to come into their diverse manifestations, each one responding to the same sunlight. Everything bursts into bloom, and yet the sun is not concerned with flowers or water, with clouds or rain. But because of the sun, all life-forms come into dynamic manifestation.

In the same way, once we realize our wholeness, we are no longer individual caretakers of any particular aspect of existence. So powerful and great is the manifestation, presence, and life force of those whose role it is to be the servants of that totality.

Brahman, the Supreme Reality, alone is real.
Beyond gender, beyond opposites,
and in whose presence,
through consciousness and mind,

the play of interrelated opposites is danced.
But Brahman itself
is not held inside that play of phenomena.
Brahman is the Supreme Reality, untouched.
It is Brahman, and when it projects itself
as the instrument
through which duality may manifest,
it still cannot leave its own Self.

Brahman is not directly concerned
with male or female, left or right, balance or imbalance.
It knows nothing of all this.
All this is for humans, not for God,
who is beyond all concerns.

It is completely beyond:
a beyond-ness of subtlety, not of distance;
for as the mind becomes more subtle
and the consciousness more refined,
conceptual transactions cease.
Speculations, projections, and interpretations end.
There remains only pure impersonal perception
arising in the majesty of Being.

As we merge with Brahman
through perfect understanding,
all duality ends.
No longer is there any sense of an entity
that needs to determine anything.
We are wholeness and move as Unity.

Over the millennia,
so many beings have searched for Truth,
for the root of their own existence,
and now their bodies have perished.
Now it's *our* turn to live in the search for Truth.
By prioritizing that quest, we place ourselves
on the cutting edge of the human experience.

Will we find that which is imperishable,
inexhaustible, timeless, and indestructible
—that which we truly are?

Transcending Our Conditioning

THE IDEA WE HAVE of who we are shapes the world we perceive and the way we see ourselves and others. People generally believe that the way they view the world is the correct way to see things. But is the idea we have of who we are or of the world as we know it really factual?

If it were factual, then whatever you take to be true would also hold true for everyone else. But that doesn't tally with our experience. In much the same way that you cannot share a dream with anyone, even by describing it—as the sharing of words about it does not amount to sharing the intimate experience of the dream—so too our waking life is uniquely our own.

From a personal standpoint, the world will never agree upon anything. At the level of the body-mind and the personality, there will always be disagreement within every nation, every tribe, and even every household, because the mind's waves and the streams of interpretation are unique. We can never be identical in our perception of anything.

People often say that we must become like one big family. But is it just a spiritual fantasy that we are capable of coming together as one world in which people love one another?

To begin with, very few people in the world really want humanity to be one family. The lives of many people are dedicated to making sure that universal love and cooperation do not happen: "We don't want them to join us! We have the advantage, so why should we share with them?"

Universal, all-embracing love is not possible to attain through the mind; it can only happen through the heart. And to be in the heart, we have to go beyond the limitations of the personality and the conditioned self.

I often say that you must be the cow that jumped over the moon. I grew up with this nursery rhyme: "Hey diddle-diddle, the cat and the fiddle, the cow jumped over the moon—" Can you be *the cow that jumps over the moon*? What is the moon? It's your mind. Trust that what may seem impossible to your mind is totally possible for the innermost Being. You have to go beyond the functioning of the body-mind, because nothing is stable in that realm. You must jump over your moon-mind. You must jump out of this realm totally. And when you come out, you come into a realization of the place that you have always been.

Sometimes you have to be challenged to do something that you as a person cannot do. Otherwise, all your progress will remain limited to the mind. If you stay just as the person, the mind will become a minefield—*boom!*

You are neither the person nor the mind. These are just movements inside a greater awareness. I am turning you back toward awareness—your purest Being, your purest Self.

Transcending Cultural Conditioning

Cultural conditioning shapes who we think we are at any given point in our lives. Few are those who ever challenge or outgrow the beliefs that have been instilled by family and society during those early years. Only when we are again established in our heart's center may we be called a universal being. Until then everyone is tribal. People belong to tribes of cultural norms that not only impose particular expectations and inhibitions on them but also foster certain ambitions in them. Being the awareness widens our sense of being. We no longer feel inclined to stay put in this highly localized self and its narrow ideas. Our being is size-less, but through acculturation it got crammed into a tight shape. Now I am releasing the straps of that straightjacket.

That one you may call a Christ, a Buddha, or a Krishna has gone beyond all conditioning. But those beings were flesh and blood just like us. They enjoyed looking at the same moon and the smell of lavender, just like you. So what was different about them? Only that they transcended the limitations of conditioning, including the root conditioning of being a person, and awoke from the hypnosis of all that seemed to stand in the way of Self-discovery.

When I speak of cultural conditioning, I want to acknowledge that not all conditioning is bad. Indeed, it is also unavoidable—just like all the fish in the ocean are wet, all the beings in the world are conditioned. Some conditioning can be positive. I could say that about certain aspects of my own conditioning, such as respecting the elderly, being kind to others, and embracing the teachings of Christ. These are forms of conditioning that I am glad to have received.

However, many bad habits and false ideas have been engrained in us in the course of our upbringing, and we became attached to those ideas. When it comes time to really go beyond the boundaries of your cultural conditioning, those ideas tend to stick to you like Velcro. You want to shake them off, but they aren't going anywhere. In your mind, you may say that you want to be rid of them, but attachment holds your mind back. Then you can go to someone who has actually done it who can show you the easy way through what seems impossible. It is for this purpose that satsang has come to play its part in the great game called life—not to replace cultural conditioning with spiritual conditioning, but in order for you to recognize your inherent limitless nature.

The most effective way to transcend cultural limitations is to go back to the place of awareness. Rather than focusing on being universal, instead discover awareness itself. Then you will automatically be in your universality, and no longer will you be crippled by any kind of conditioning.

WE ARE PERCEIVING WHAT WE ARE CONCEIVING. IF YOUR CONCEPTIONS ARE BASED UPON AND LIMITED BY CULTURAL PARADIGMS, THEN YOU ARE LIVING IN A KIND OF RUT.

One can climb high and go far within the paradigm of a particular culture. But if, at the end of the day, you're still left with the idea of *us* and *them*, then you haven't completed your seeing, because pure consciousness, pure awareness, is beyond all categories. It's not even a belief that you have moved beyond cultural biases. It's just that you're open to other points of view because you have the ability to enter different modes of consciousness and perceive how things look from different angles. It is a very compassionate way of living when you can understand how people see things from their various perspectives. And when people manifest the distortions of culturally limited thinking, even if you don't speak up and challenge them about it or try to guide them to a more universal point of view, the openness of your heart and the spaciousness of your Being will affect them enormously.

Once you have discovered the place of awareness as your Self, your true nature still expresses itself in its own unique way and may retain some flavor of the localization of consciousness that we call culture. Cultures have their beauty, and all are part of the dance of life. All have their place in the great tapestry of the manifest world. This is beautiful, but not when only that one perspective is known.

You must come to know the ground, the root, the very womb from which all cultures are born and take their expression—and that womb is not different from your own Self. I am happy not only to be saying this but also to be seeing this realization flourish. It's not that we are asking people to go out and speak about this. No, just *be* that. You *are* that! As you discover your essential nature, it happens automatically that the beingness broadens and becomes panoramic in its seeing.

We are perceiving what we are conceiving. If your conceptions are based upon and limited by cultural paradigms, then you are living in a kind of rut. As an outcome of remaining in this groove of seeing, you are probably going to perceive other cultural paradigms as being somehow off track. The very contrast is often seen as opposition, and conflicts are born of that tendency.

The one who has transcended the field of duality has come into a most gracious field—the discovery of the universal Self, pure awareness itself. I am very happy for this. It is as if the world of the manifest existed primarily in the realm of the mind, and even in its highest expression—the cosmic mind, one may say—that kingdom is still connected to our minds. But awareness is beyond all categories and qualities. In fact, it is at the heart of all qualities.

What could be a greater joy to discover?

Moving Beyond Religious Tribalism

We have been conditioned not only by the cultural expectations of our societies, but also by the influences of religion on those cultures. As with national or ethnic identity, one can also say that every religion is a tribe. Is there anything wrong with that? No. Each form of religious expression has emerged out of our human culture. One could say that it is the one Supreme Being manifesting them all out of compassion to cater to each people according to that culture's particular temperament. In these myriad cultural expressions, you can see the great religious rivers of life, of believers and nonbelievers, all flowing toward the great sea of the ineffable Self.

But all religions *are* tribes, nonetheless. What is felt to be miraculous to Christians may not be appealing to Muslims or Buddhists or atheists. Yet everyone says, or at least implies, "Ours is the best." That's like saying, "Chinese food is the best!" Well, you might think that if you are Chinese, but then the Italians will come along and say, "What about pizza?!"

It would be wrong—indeed, it would be appalling—if there were ever to be only one religion in the world. It would be the biggest fascist undertaking you could ever imagine. We need all the religions for as long as the human race still needs to be educated. Each religion shows us something else and from a different angle, so that our development and our understanding can become universal.

I want to encourage people toward a more universal view. We have been brought up in our own traditions, and nobody is free of the biases those traditions have imparted. Our conditioning—especially our spiritual conditioning—is tribal. When we apply ourselves only to the personal realm, we cannot get over our biases so easily; it is as if they were running in our veins and we were breathing them in our lungs. Yet, I'm not saying that this transcendence is going to be difficult. No, it's actually easier from the place of awareness, because awareness has nothing to transcend. The greatest and most beautiful things in life are always easier, because the universal is far more natural than the personal.

IN THESE MYRIAD CULTURAL EXPRESSIONS, YOU CAN SEE THE GREAT RELIGIOUS RIVERS OF LIFE, OF BELIEVERS AND NONBELIEVERS, ALL FLOWING TOWARD THE GREAT SEA OF THE INEFFABLE SELF.

Every religion is, in some way, incomplete in the way that it is generally understood by its followers. You cannot understand the Truth when it is only partial and biased: "*We* found the Truth, but as for the Muslims . . ." This idea isn't true. If you feel that you have realized the Truth as a Buddhist, a Christian, a Jew, or a Muslim but the other religions are "not quite there," then you have not realized the Truth. The pure Self is to be found at the very heart of each religion. From that core essence, every one of the religions points a finger toward Truth, but the finger itself is not the point—no, you must follow the pointing!

Being part of a tribe is okay, but you must go beyond it inwardly. You are the Self, and the Self is universal. Truth is beyond religion. Religion at its best just facilitates the recognition of Truth. Being religious is not the goal. When you realize the Truth of your own Self, you will have transcended all tribal limitations. You are not against anyone. In fact, you are *for* all of existence because you are one with it.

How beautiful.

Melt in the Ocean of Unity

Three little beings found themselves living on a beach. Although they had always lived and played there at the edge of the ocean, they didn't know how they had gotten there. They looked like small dolls. One of them was made of water, another was made of sand, and the third, of salt.

One stormy night, they all dreamed vivid dreams that seemed to stick with them when they awoke in the morning. When they saw one another, they were all uncharacteristically introspective. Noticing that the others were also pensive, each asked the other, "What's wrong?"

The water doll said to the sand doll, "I don't know. It's just that I had this dream . . ."

"You too?" replied the sand doll. "I also had a strange dream."

Now the third one, the salt doll said, "This is pretty odd! I too had an unusual dream!"

"So, what was your dream?" they all said excitedly to one another at the same time.

The salt doll then said, "I dreamed that I came from this ocean."

"Was I talking in my sleep?" said the sand doll. "I too dreamed that I was that ocean, that I've always been here, as old as the ocean itself."

The water doll said, "You guys must be joking! I must have been the one talking in my sleep and you two heard me, because I also dreamed that I came directly from the ocean!"

Incredulous, they looked at one another and all said at once, "Oh my God, do you mean that we are all from the ocean? But we look so different! I wonder which one of us is *most* like the ocean?"

Oh, they were so very excited; now it was a competition!

The sand doll said, "I feel that I am most like the ocean. Look, there's sand everywhere!"

The water doll said, "No, no, look at all of this—it's me. Just look at the water!"

Then the salt doll said, "No competition! Just stick your tongues out, and it tastes of what?—me, salt!"

"How can we test who is most like the ocean?" they all asked in unison.

"We have to go in!"

Now, they were very playful beings indeed, and all wanted to go first. So they drew straws to decide. The first to go was the water doll. She had wings, so she flew up so high as to almost become invisible, and then, right over the ocean, she plunged into the water—*shtook!*—and that was that.

The other two dolls were waiting. "Why is she taking so long? It's my turn! Where is she? Maybe she decided to explore a bit, as the ocean is so vast."

Finally, the salt doll said, "I can't wait! I'll go see where she is. If she comes back, tell her I went after her."

So off she went in her nice little dress and hat. She started to walk out on the surface of the water, but as she went, each part of her body that touched the water disappeared: the little feet, the knees, and the arms. As she went, all melted into the ocean so that, finally, only a little salt hat was left floating on the surface, then—*phumph!*—the hat too was gone.

The water doll did not come back, and neither did the salt doll. So the sand doll said, "I don't know if I like this game! How long should it take? We haven't even had breakfast yet. I think I'll go take a nap on the beach because nobody seems to be coming back for now."

The day passed and the evening passed too, and the sand doll slept contentedly. The moon rose and the tide came up, and she was still there sleeping. Slowly the waves lapped up and took her tiny toes and feet, then her legs and hips—*whoosh!*—finally her little fingers.

In the end, there was no one left to say who was most like the ocean.

Each doll represents a certain kind of temperament embodied in a religion or a spiritual way. Let the dolls play until they melt away. Each seeker who truly investigates into their own essence will melt here in that ocean of unity.

Breaking the Spell of Personhood

There is nothing that you need to accomplish in order to be what you are. What you are is already established effortlessly and time-lessly. However, this is something that we need to recognize and confirm, as that is how we break the spell or hypnosis of personhood that causes us to believe that we are other than what we truly are.

Unless we are aware of the natural state of being, we always seem to be experiencing some sense of background agitation. Especially in the Western culture, we are always running restlessly about, fueled by the feeling that we always have to be in gear.

Once you become aware of your 'I-am-ness,' you are at peace. When people speak to you, it is the 'I-am-ness' that energetically does the listening and spontaneously responds. You, as a person, don't have to do it. The person is a very busy character, while the 'I-am-ness' is never busy, even if it does many things. As presence, one comes to see that all activities are carried out by the vital energy that resides in the body.

We will only come to understand what it means to be in the natural, neutral state once we are really ready to enter that state. If I were to say, "Don't do anything," you might instead *try* to do nothing, which would be ridiculous. So I don't advise you to *do nothing*. Rather, let your activities occur naturally and keep your attention in the 'I am.'

If you make the mistake of believing that activities disturb the state of presence, then you will start avoiding them. But activities are simply unfolding in the 'I am,' which is the witness of them all, so being active will no longer disturb you. It's something very natural.

You might ask, "Is it enough if I'm just okay with things as they come?" And I say, nothing will be enough until you are stabilized in your Being. When you are stable here, then whatever arises will naturally correspond with your Being. You will no longer be a person trying to do something. But as long as that personal sense remains in control, it will always be scratching about. It will be dissatisfied even with the 'I am' presence.

It will say, "I don't get this 'I-am-ness' thing.
I'd better go do something else!"
So it will start chanting *Om namah shivaya*
until it falls asleep.
It will walk up a holy mountain until it is exhausted.
Then it will come down and bathe in the Ganges
until it gets cold.
And then it will start to sing devotional hymns
until it is tired of that as well.

As long as the person keeps "trying to get there," it will get fed up with every state. But as you pay attention—and you can begin today—you will become aware of that natural feeling 'I am.' And you don't have to go out looking for it. In fact, to go looking for it would be a mistake, because then you are already being duped by the mind's tricks. You *are* the 'I am.'

How natural, how simple this truth is!

Truth Takes No Time

The 'I' has, by force of habit, been given over to the ego and mind so that we behave as if the personal sense is all we are. But it is not; it can *behave* as though it were, it can *believe* itself to be, but essentially, the small self is not our ultimate reality. 'I' means presence, holy presence. It can never *not* be true. It can only be dreamed to be something else. Satsang is that space in which you can confirm for yourself that this presence is true, and that affirmation brings you great joy and peace.

Many beings are looking for ways to stabilize in this joy and peace. Such an urge seems sincere and credible, but I always say, first find out who wants to stabilize there. Don't miss this point. Presence itself is already stable. But something is still believing in and identifying with the questioner who asks, "How can I become stabilized in presence?" Already the language demonstrates a sense of separation.

Where did this sense of distance come from anyway? It grew out of conditioning and from identifying with the sense of personhood. This imagined division between yourself and God—between yourself and Truth—is the single most toxic belief one can embrace, because it poisons everything else. If you believe that something is fundamentally wrong with you, then you will always be trying to work on yourself, always trying to fix what's "broken."

I am pointing out that the very belief in duality is ill conceived. But something inside you is still loyal to the old self-doubting identity: "I'm not sure I get it. He must be speaking in riddles or Zen koans." We are going to burn all this nonsense out so that such language and thoughts will not trouble you anymore.

It's not that once you awaken to the Self you will start to speak like some divine voice that booms out, "I am the 'I am'!" But there *will* be a new fragrance emanating from your presence, because you will have arrived home again where you can thrive. This life is for winning your freedom back from its captivity in delusion.

You might ask, "Can this happen for me right now?" Presence itself is already perfect. So, what you are asking is whether the one who is imperfect—which itself is only an idea—can somehow drop itself so that it sees that what remains is its natural Self. As long as you continue to identify as that 'me' for whom it would happen, then it may take some time.

But the Truth takes no time. Presence is timelessly here; it just may take some time for you to discover the timeless because the mind is mischievous. Belief structures get created, and we have to somehow dismantle them to deconstruct the myths. Something like a reflex makes us jump back to personal identity. It is this draining away of untruth that may take some time.

Over the millennia, so many beings have searched for Truth, for the root of their own existence, and now their bodies have perished. Now it's *our turn* to live in the search for Truth. By prioritizing that quest, we place ourselves on the cutting edge of the human experience. Will we find that which is imperishable, inexhaustible, timeless, and indestructible—that which we truly are?

Let us use our time to discover the timeless. Let the timebound be with you as well, but don't try to grab onto it. Time says,

"All of this that you perceive, on the outside of the
eyes and even behind the eyes in the realm of emotion,
thought, memory, and imagination, even the very place
where concepts themselves are born—all of that belongs
to *me*. I am time, and I will take all of it with me. Also,
if you're not careful, I'll take *you* with me as well!"

Time even eats entire civilizations and buries them beneath
the earth. Some ancient kingdoms are buried so deep that only
archaeologists can find them, digging them out with great effort
because time has devoured and buried them. Every name, every
form you see, time will change, eat, and swallow. But time also
says, "I will eat everything you perceive, but awareness, I cannot
eat. Awareness will eat me."

There is something that time cannot take. Until you realize
this timelessness as your true Being, time will take everything
you think you have and all that you think you are.

Your beingness came here to resolve itself in oneness.

So, be *That*. What need have you for anything else?

Merge with the Infinite

Even though it is not true that we're simply the sum of our thoughts,
most beings experience life as if they are. You are consciousness, this
space in which thoughts manifest and are perceived. This immaculate immensity is what we are. It isn't something to be learned.
Rather, one recognizes and merges with, in, and as That itself. Paradoxically, it is the inquiry that enables this profound recognition
and conviction inside the heart of being, though the nature of the
Self—which is without qualities—rests beyond the inquiry.

The mind is afraid of the idea of merging with the Infinite, because at present it is functioning as a composite, personal self held together by concepts and feelings within a physical body. The fear arises that to merge means the dissolution of our identity and form. But the very fear of dissolution is a sign that the unreal is vanishing. It's a sign of the unfolding recognition of your limitless Self.

The mind acts as a veil, as a fog of ignorance and arrogance, to this intuitive recognition of unchanging awareness. It is ever calculating, always trying to navigate rather than just flowing as life itself. As long as you continue navigating in this way, nearly blind, the sharp odor of agitation will be your scent. You will miss the obvious perfection of existence.

Can you see without passing judgment? Can you just perceive neutrally? When you see things in such neutrality, you see them as they really are. You have no more need for judgment because you are seeing from the Self. Often we watch life reactively, creating our own story as we go along. But is it possible to just *see* without forming biases or preferences?

It is exhausting to perceive the world in the reactive and judgmental mode in which most people function. They exhaust themselves in the notion that they are living life rather than realizing that they *are* life itself.

In the space of impersonal panoramic perceiving, there is no judgment and there are no personal reactions. Because ego is absent, there is just seeing. This state is much less exhausting, and one finds that far less sleep is needed than ever before. But the mind objects: "No, no! Less sleep?! You're putting me to sleep right now! This so-called state of equanimity is so dull. Life should be passionate!"

In the energy field of satsang, you have a taste of how it feels to inhabit this body when you are no longer in service to your mind. How easy and naturally life flows! How our horizons expand when we are no longer contracted or anxious. When you are absent in a personal way, how light, spacious, and generous your beingness is! It is a simple thing really; you are not easily disturbed, and there are no habitual or lingering judgments, fears, or anxieties. You move in grace. Life is serene and unfolds as a state of radiant presence in motion. This state of Being is emanating out of the silence of the true Self.

IN THE SPACE OF IMPERSONAL PANORAMIC PERCEIVING, THERE IS NO JUDGMENT AND THERE ARE NO PERSONAL REACTIONS. BECAUSE EGO IS ABSENT, THERE IS JUST SEEING.

Truth is not a creation. Removing the false, therefore, does not create the Truth; it just removes what prevented the Truth from being recognized.

You, as consciousness, have the capacity to contemplate the highest reality. Once you come to see this reality, you realize that your actions are the actions of the universe, not of an individual. Even when you are identified as a person, your actions are the actions of the universe, operating through the mind in much the same way that each wave has the complete and total ocean beneath it. Every wave has its origin in the ocean, and so it is the movement of the ocean. But you are the ocean, not just a wave!

All impulses and actions are only waves arising out of your oceanic Being. It is *you* who sees them rather than them seeing you. They have no existence apart from you, the perceiver of mind-waves. Acknowledge and be one with this knowing and observe the waves of illumination that arise out of your oceanic Self.

The mind makes the realization of the Self into a struggle of "getting there," but it's not about getting there or becoming anything.

You are *already* the ineffable Self. You simply need to recognize, confirm, and verify your real position as the observing source, the emptiness from which all phenomena arise.

Emptiness is only another word for what you are. You spend your whole life trying to be the best 'someone' you can be, but now you are discovering that you are actually no one. This is the most significant and profound discovery a human being can make, and in this discovery is true freedom, true joy, and true peace.

There are no references for such a one who is unborn awareness. It is simple, unique, original, yet beyond the concept of unique and original; it is pure Self-consciousness in the truest sense. The observing source that is earlier than mind is the true sage within you. If, accompanied and guided by that inner sage, you were to undertake a journey from which you could never return, how would you feel about completing it? What if you could just continue ever deepening in wisdom and insight, while thinning away as a personal identity, free-falling into the state of blissful emptiness? What could be the threat here? What do you stand to lose? You can lose everything else, but you can never lose the awareness that you are. It is the consciousness of Being and Self-awareness that we love. This awareness is supreme, for it does not depend on anything perceivable.

> *You* are the sage whom you seek.
> You are the treasure trove of wisdom
> that cannot be defined or described.
> The wind blows, but no one knows
> from where it comes, nor where it will go.
> It is the same with the sagely presence—
> unpredictable, auspicious, and untraceable.

The more attention you give to examining your conditioning
and asking what still needs to be flushed out from beingness,
the more you actually create the conditions
for this stuff to come alive and grow like mold.

You say, "I want to be done with it."
But do yourself a favor:
don't bother trying to pick off
thoughts one by one.

Such an approach is like trying to prune
a great banyan tree one leaf at a time.
By the time you think that you have come to the last leaf,
new ones are already growing behind you.

The Person's Work Is Never Done

THE LIGHT OF THE SELF is always present. It is the source of all manifestation. In this sense, you are always the Self. But unless the direct recognition of our true nature takes place in you, you are not yet the Self. In being truly awake, you are conscious of your timelessness. You are conscious of life as the unity of the All-ness experienced beyond time-bound phenomena. You live in and as *That*.

What a seeming paradox: we are already perfect, yet something needs to be recognized for us to awaken to our inherent perfection.

Be aware that when I say that you are already perfect, it is not that I am giving you a compliment. I am not showing you that you are perfect in the way the mind would like—you are not perfect *as a person*. Rather, discover this timeless perfection that is your original Being. Then, *you* show *me*!

You have to discover this Truth for yourself. Then you will know that its power is not just a theory and that it's not a hoax. And I don't want to delay your realization of this Truth.

No, you are this *today*.

Something inside of you may respond, "Well, I don't feel it!" But even feeling it is not enough. You must come to know it in your heart. I am always pointing you toward that nonphenomenal recognition.

Are You Already Rich?

Once upon a time there were two middle-aged men who had been close friends ever since childhood. They were the kind of friends who tell each other *everything*, even things they could not tell their own families.

One man told the other, "You are my most trusted friend. I want to tell you a secret in case something should happen to me. I have come into a great deal of money from an investment and have buried this money under the house. I am reluctant to tell my wife, because she is not wise with money, and I have not told my son, because he is already spoiled."

Soon after, the rich man's trusted confidant went traveling and only returned to his hometown after several years. To his surprise, he came across his friend's wife and son on the street one day, begging and scrounging in bins for food. Aghast, he went up to her and said, "Sister, do you remember me?"

She looked up and said, "Of course! You are my husband's best friend!"

"What are you doing begging and scavenging?"

"Don't you know? My husband suddenly passed away two years ago. We had enough money for a while, but now I have to beg on the street just so we can eat. Thank God, at least we still have our house."

Then he said, "I must tell you something. Before I left to go traveling, your husband confided in me that he had left a lot of money for you. He hesitated to tell you at the time, because he feared you would not spend it wisely. He asked me to tell you about it when the time was right."

Even upon just hearing the news, mother and son were already ecstatic, because they knew they could trust this person.

They had but heard the news from his mouth, and already they no longer felt like poor people.

Then he said, "Come, come, I'll show you. We mustn't delay. You've passed enough time being poor! Let us dig up that treasure chest!" So they went to the house, pulled up the floorboards, and began to dig. Soon—*thud!*—they hit something. Their hearts were pounding as they unearthed the box, pulled it out, unlatched it, threw it open, and—lo and behold—it was brimming with money.

Now this treasure had been there on her property since before her husband's death, so it had always been hers. But before unearthing the treasure, were she and her son rich? No. The hidden treasure had always been there, but they were unaware of it, so they had no access to what that treasure could have made possible.

We are like that woman and her son. We are free. We have always been free. We are none other than this pure, perfect Being, even though we may not yet be conscious of this. Some amount of trust is necessary, as there are forces working to distract you. It is part of the game of consciousness that it should not be too easy to find the treasure that is already yours; if it were too easy, you might not value it.

Some people may ask, "Why should we have to go through all this? If we are perfect, why haven't we been able to manifest this perfection?" Well, we *are* perfect, but somehow we're all in this dream of maya together, and we are attached to this dream. We want to keep dreaming even while we wish to awaken.

The Theater of Consciousness

When we speak about Self-realization, the metaphor of awakening is apt, because we all know what it is to dream. If we dream that we are dying of thirst in a desert with a scorching sun, that sun seems totally real. The fear seems real, as does the thirst and the longing for a miracle to save us. When we wake up, though, all of it is gone, instantly! We immediately recognize this state as having been a dream.

Each day, the consciousness revolves through three states: the deep sleep, dreaming, and waking states. The waking state is what we refer to as "our life." However, this life and all that you experience, including the sense of yourself, is only the content and the play of the waking state.

If your name is John, you cannot be John twenty-four hours a day. For when deep sleep comes, even the sense 'I am' subsides, and with it goes consciousness of body and mind. In deep sleep you are not a Muslim, Christian, Jew, or Hindu, nor are you a man or a woman—nothing is there with you in deep sleep. But a subtle form of consciousness must remain even in deep sleep for you to know about this state. And everybody enjoys deep sleep. We even buy the best mattresses in order to enter this state where we forget everything.

What does this show us? It shows us that even that beautiful state of presence—that consciousness that shines inside this body as the sense 'I am' and functions as the impartial observer of the manifestation of life—is not the ultimate reality.

When you begin to reflect a little bit about these things, a deeper understanding emerges about what we call our self and life. You will come to see for yourself that this waking-state consciousness itself is also phenomenal—it is also seen.

Every morning we wake up from our dreams, but to be truly awake, we must also awaken from the waking state.

The waking state—our daily life—is like a theater of consciousness in which you appear on stage as one of the actors in this play called *Life*. All that you call your life belongs to this show that runs for sixteen hours a day. At 6:00 a.m. the alarm rings: Lights on! Show starts! You don't question who you were in deep sleep at 5:59 a.m. The sense of 'I' arises, and somehow you pick up the 'me' again: "Oh, yes, here I am. I'm an executive with an important meeting today. I can do this." Throughout the day you interact with others, you laugh, cry, and get scared, but much like an audience watching a play, you also watch yourself apparently doing all these things.

Can we really be both actor and audience to life's unfolding at the same time? Yes, but first we have to become aware of our true position in all of this as the untouched observer.

Pure observing without self-interest is what characterizes the Self, and that is the understanding of those who have become established in true Self-knowledge. In the light of pure Self-awareness, one still experiences life and the sense of 'you' and 'me,' but now the impact of this sense of duality becomes more superficial in its effect.

The neutral, uninvolved witnessing of all that arises in our daily waking state is what I call *presence*, and the person itself is witnessed inside presence. Much spiritual practice, or sadhana, is to bring the beingness that is identified as person back to its natural state of presence. The final step—which is not a step at all, but rather a nonphenomenal recognition—is that the natural sense 'I am' or 'I exist' is also phenomenal to the ultimate seeing.

Rare is the one who comes beyond this stateless state of 'I am' into the realm wherefrom even the 'I am' presence is observed. There we are in the Unspeakable, the wordless Truth, which is our absolute reality.

I don't want you to believe this. I want you to be this.

Belief Must Become Reality

Belief may be helpful in opening your heart and moving forward to embrace the Truth fully, but it's not an end in itself. Belief must become reality. Truth must be recognized, felt, authenticated, and verified through your own inner experience. This is possible today. Why? Because what you are searching for is already here. It is not something you can create, nor is it a trophy to be awarded at the end of some striving. You must recognize it as reality.

PURE OBSERVING WITHOUT SELF-INTEREST IS WHAT CHARACTERIZES THE SELF.

Mind is like the wind; your real Self is like space. The nature of the wind is to blow about, but it needs space in which to do that. You know of the wind only through the effects that you see, feel, and hear when there is something in its way. Similarly, you know of the mind only because identity is there. Space doesn't move about; it is present everywhere. Space can be without the wind, but the wind cannot be without space. The wind is always blowing in different directions. Can anyone determine which way the wind will blow? Whatever direction that may be, it can never move outside of space.

Similarly, it is not possible for you to ever move away from your Self. When you know this so profoundly that it becomes a kind of knowing beyond thought, then you are free. You can move as you will because you cannot move out of your Self. That which is moving is temporary in nature. You are the unmoving within the moving, experiencing the sense of moving. You are the invisible inside of the visible, but you also appear as the visible.

By focusing so much attention on that which is subject to change, we are still trying to care for and control something that, by nature, can never be stable. The personal identity will experience the notion of being stable for a while, and then it will be up and running again. That is the nature of the changeable. Leave it to its nature and stay as you are. Some concepts pull us into the illusion that we are just that flickering self-image, but the truth is that we simultaneously *are* and *aren't* that.

The Two Birds

Some time ago, I saw a picture depicting a parable from the Bhagavad Gita. It showed two birds in a tree, and one of them was building a nest. This one is flying off collecting things, arranging the twigs—it's active, doing many things.

Above this bird, on another branch, is a second bird. It looks identical to the first bird, but it's not building anything. It is just observing. It's not building a self-image out of its perceiving, and it's not deeply interested in any aspect of what it sees. Its perceiving is happening quite spontaneously without effort or judgment. There's a silence there, that feeling of Being without thought. Just looking.

This is a beautiful portrait of who we are.

These two birds are connected. The first bird represents our dynamic being, the self that is engaged in the world, in future and past, in growing. It is the aspect that is living life with the sense of *my family, my children, my work,* and so on. The second bird represents that conscious witnessing within us. It is the ability to observe life taking place and activities unfolding, but it is not actually doing anything. It is still within the same body, but it is not manipulating. It is not saying, "I hope this, and I fear that." No, it is very still. It is simply there, and its seeing is panoramic. It sees not only the first bird, but also the wind in the trees, the sky—everything is observed with a kind of neutrality.

Initially the first bird is very identified with building the nest. It may not even be aware of the second bird. But as soon as it is able to be quiet, it becomes aware of the second bird, which is actually itself at a deeper inner level. When the first bird's mind is synchronized with the second bird, the activities become much more gracious. There is a sense of a unity, a oneness. In that harmony, the work may still happen but without obsession, without fear, without the sense of needing to control things. It is simply happening because life compels this activity to happen. It is as though another power is helping the actions to take place.

BECAUSE THERE IS STILL IDENTITY WITH THIS SENSE OF *I AM THE DOER,* THAT SINGULAR MISTAKE BEGETS AND THEN FEEDS A HUNDRED OTHER MISTAKES.

The second bird represents the change of perspective from the mode of the person to the state of presence. When we are involved in the activities of life so deeply that it seems that the daily routine is all there is, then we are like this first bird, the nest builder, oblivious to our second bird position.

Come to the second bird position, to the one who is observing, and you will discover that the one who is busy building a life will slowly become more transparent, leaving only the functioning itself. The activities are happening anyway, beautifully, but the sense of doer-ship—which is the ego sense—will fade away. Activities are just happening; our self-image as a person is just happening, but our true Self is not a happening. In fact, the true Self is a third position, which is not a bird, but the space within which both birds are arising and seen.

If you come to see and accept what I am pointing to, and if you can slow down just a bit, your witnessing will become very serene, and you will notice that the activities of life are just happening by themselves.

The wind doesn't say, "I'm going to blow this tree!" So it is that your thoughts and the sense that "I must do this or that" are just happening. But because there is still identity with this sense of *I am the doer*, that singular mistake begets and then feeds a hundred other mistakes.

You can discover the Truth of who you are, and you can do it now. What gets in your way? Your loyalty to the old regime of thinking, to the habit and idea of continuing on as who you were yesterday and who you were last month. It may also seem like a big risk to accept something that might be too transformative. You may feel, *I can only handle so much.* And this thought seems to be deeply held.

You want so much but offer so little of yourself in return. Thirsty, you want to drink deeply, but you come to the fountain with a teaspoon in your hand.

You may ask, "Are you telling me that I don't have to do anything in particular, and that I am already That?"

"Yes," I reply.

You say, "But how can I be That when my mind is full of nonsense and screaming?"

"Let it scream," I respond.

"But I'm sure the Buddha didn't have a screaming mind," you object.

I say, "How do you know that the Buddha didn't have a screaming mind, but simply ignored it?"

Please understand that ignoring thoughts does not mean trying to stop or suppress thoughts. Simply turn away from them. Some thoughts, however, keep showing up no matter where you turn. They seem to have a season pass for your attention. This is when I tell you: what you cannot ignore, simply observe.

The Purpose of Observing

At this point, let me clarify that if you are just observing mechanically, you have not understood what it really means to observe, and one way or another you are going to get pulled back into the scene again. What is the purpose of observing? The instruction to observe is given so that you verify, and thus clarify, that whatever you may be seeing or experiencing is merely transient. It cannot be who you are. In the moment you are looking at the turbulent mind, it certainly *seems* real enough. The effects in their highest pulsation feel so intimately connected with who you take yourself to be, it is as if they were the very lifeblood flowing through your veins and the very air moving in your lungs. Still this isn't sufficient evidence that any of it is real. Because in a moment or two, that breath of egoic identity has already been exhaled, and the screaming mind has already passed.

Just hold your ground as the undivided seer.

Identity Implies I-Entity

Any habitual or persistent problems or emotions are growing a person, an 'I-me,' underneath them. This is why I say, where there is identity, it implies an I-entity.

If there is a bad smell in the room, you can engage your sense of smell—*Aha! It smells like gas*—and then you follow it until you find the gas leak. In much the same way that we can follow a bad smell to its source, we can use strong emotions such as anger, guilt, fear, a restless mind, and so forth to sniff out the identity. Whatever the circumstances that bring up personal identity for you, use the energetic presence of that particular feeling in the body to see if you can find the I-entity who feels impacted by what is happening.

Whatever the feeling, look inward and inquire: Can an actual I-entity be found? Who is suffering, and who is complaining? Can the guilty party be found and presented?

Turn your attention inward and just keep quiet.

Don't add any opinions to the inquiry.

Don't change the question, and beware of the mind's tendency to become distracted.

Just try to cleanly identify the one who is disturbed or suffering.

Can it be perceived?

Can you find a suffering 'I'?

Is it tangible?

Could it be that the felt sense of an I-entity is merely a sensation that has become clothed in identity—as *who I am*—that, in fact, there is nobody there who is suffering?

For thousands of years, beings have been looking for this one, for this 'person,' the actual sufferer, but no one has been able to find this one as a tangible entity.

And the one who is making this discovery—that there is actually nobody there to suffer—can *that* one be found?

Turning the attention inward and scanning one's sense of being for the 'I-me' sense burns all delusions and brings you to a non-finding discovery, thus revealing your true Self.

For most people, mental activity has become compulsive—an addiction and an affliction, a chattering voice that simply won't stop. Self-inquiry should not be done mentally. It is not just repeating, "Who am I? Who am I? Who am I?" with the hope that an answer or object will appear as the Self. You have to actually look! And do not hold a preconceived idea of what you may find. The inquiry has to be fresh each time. Don't wait or harbor expectations—not even expectations based on the memory of what happened the last time you inquired or of that beautiful glimpse that you had some time ago. No, you have to be fresh! That is why my advice is to remain only in that timeless neutrality of awareness. Your neutrality will neutralize everything and bring it back to its fundamental, essential nature.

> YOUR NEUTRALITY WILL NEUTRALIZE EVERYTHING AND BRING IT BACK TO ITS FUNDAMENTAL, ESSENTIAL NATURE.

What will happen as you let go of obsessive control is that delusions will disappear, as will the fog of depression, the sense of displacement, worry about the future, the fear of death, and the fear of life. All of this will be history when we embrace the full potential of our Being.

Only grace can bring you to this freedom, to this inner tranquility. And grace won't keep you waiting. In nature, you may wait for rain. Are you like that? Like dry land waiting for rain? There is something you don't have to wait for because it is already here, and it is at the root of who you are. This is the great news. You have to wait for everything else: to get married, to have children, to get a good job, to get paid your wages—you even have to wait for dinner. But grace is something that you don't have to wait for.

There is a saying of Saint Francis of Assisi,

What you are looking *for*
is already where you are looking *from*.

And Rumi says,

Knocking on a door. It opens.
I've been knocking from the inside.

Both are big clues and profound pointers to the Truth of who we are. So why does it seem like a riddle? Because we just cannot believe that it could possibly be so simple. It only becomes supremely difficult because we want to achieve emptiness with the unstable and changeful mind.

Hardship Is Not Necessary

Self-realization is not about, "I have to eat only nuts and berries while living naked in a cave until I realize the Self." But people hold onto such monumental ideals and believe things like *no-pain-no-gain*. Look how much hardship spiritual seekers have inflicted upon themselves. While it may be an expression that some need to go through, in general it's not necessary.

Discovering your true nature doesn't require that you suffer hardships or give up the things you enjoy.

All that you see in life emerges from the womb of God. God is beyond *us* and *them*, *like* and *dislike*. And yet that very duality can be enjoyed by everyone when we see it in the correct way. Duality can be playful, but if you take yourself to be only an individual person, your experience in life is going to be intense—or even tragic or cruel.

There's nothing you can look at here in life, especially in your inner life, that could be said to be a fact. Everything exists in the realm of possibility, and the quality and content of your inner life will be determined by who *you* are who perceives it. Nothing in life has a single inherent meaning; rather, it will have different meanings for different beings according to their conditioning, identity, and so on. None of it is stable, but all is the functioning of consciousness nonetheless.

You simultaneously act in your play and are its most attentive audience, being moved by the story, intrigued by the plot, and also critical of the acting and scripting. One day you merge with the pure observer and transcend both the role of actor and that of the critical audience. Then you and life are one. When you become empty of ego, you will move through this world happily and unburdened.

Dissolving the Mind's Residue

Even when you feel emptied out of person, the mind's residue might still remain inside your vessel for a while. You want to be done with it, to be immaculately clean, but it is sticky. Its stickiness corresponds to the strength of your attachment to identity.

Any residue gradually dissolves as your identification with the sense of personhood weakens. So, if you are moving ever more into the space of the Self and are letting it happen in a natural way, then these tendencies will no longer be able to exert the influence they once did.

The more attention you give to examining your conditioning and asking what still needs to be flushed out from beingness, the more you actually create the conditions for this stuff to come alive and grow like mold. You say, "I want to be done with it." But do yourself a favor: don't bother trying to pick off thoughts one by one. Such an approach may work—kind of—but it's like trying to prune a great banyan tree one leaf at a time. By the time you think that you have come to the last leaf, new ones are already growing behind you. It is a slow, exhausting, and inefficient method.

The faster and more effective way is just to remember your Self. It's a bit like going to listen to an orchestra and focusing only on the violins. If I were to ask that of you, you could do it. You wouldn't have to tell the other musicians in the orchestra to play softly in order to let only the violins be heard. No, you would just somehow attune your attention to the violins.

In much the same way, you may attune your attention to the Self. But you are only able to do this if you recognize that silence—that sublime stateless state that is the Self—so that among all the movements that occur in life, you can stay as that which is *not* moving or happening. The Self is not an object, entity, or event. Rather, it is a space-like awareness within which the changeful is experienced, but which itself remains untouched. So don't feed all these little things that come up in your mind, because that will only turn them into a story.

Remember: there are no stories in the Self.

Once you have seen something clearly in the light of inquiry, confirm it right then and there. You don't have a lot of work to do; just focus on what you are seeing. See it! When you truly see something, you won't have to keep going over already-conquered ground, which is to say that you will no longer doubt your own seeing. For instance, if you were to clearly see someone stealing something from you, would you ever entertain doubts about who the thief really was? No, you wouldn't. In much the same way, you've now looked and seen that the sense of personhood is not real. Whenever it comes back again, you will recognize this one as the thief who is attempting to rob you of your inherent peace.

Your witnessing will continue to become ever more sensitive and perceptive. Your discerning power will sharpen until the energy of the illusion of there being a person is sufficiently weakened and thus transcended. But you're not waiting for that to happen. You are not a 'someone' who is waiting. You are here, resting only in and as the timeless Self. Being one with the Self, all comes into harmony spontaneously.

If you remain as a personality, however, you will always be pressing buttons and tweaking things, for the person's work is never done!

Once you see all as consciousness, you will no longer be moving things about, chopping down trees, or putting out fires. Instead, by simply looking from your own source Being, you will understand that thoughts are just dancing images projected onto the screen of consciousness.

You see them for what they are, and you know that this seeing is not just a belief.

Look at how momentary thoughts are—here one moment, gone the next. So why fall in love with a cloud? How long can that marriage last? All phenomena are like clouds drifting by.

Don't Follow the Person-Poison

Often in satsang, people come to ask a question, and in that question I can hear that they are still strongly identified with the sense of personhood. For example, one man said he constantly saw a film of his failures running through his mind, so much so that he even dreamed about those failures. He felt guilty and unworthy and wanted to let go of those regrets.

He is not alone in this wishing; many people also feel this way. But it is only the person that says, "I am caught up in this life, but I want to be finished with it all." I don't ask you to disidentify from that person; just to be aware of the identification and to ask yourself: "What is aware of identity? Does that which is aware of 'my' story itself have a story?"

Let the personal story be there, but acknowledge that it has been granted tremendous significance and has therefore exercised a greatly negative influence over the quality of your life. Now, you may have become aware of this, but something still doesn't quite understand the significance of just being aware. What I am referring to is not an *awareness of* any thing, but rather *awareness* itself. As soon as you turn your attention to awareness, you will notice that attention is also observed *from* and *in* awareness. Few seem to value this awareness, even though it is the source of their own existence.

There is a space within you that is a kind of neutral field from where you can look at all aspects of your life. You don't even have to go out in search of them, as they will float up into view by themselves.

Learn to look, but watch out for the tendency to interpret events. Many things happen in our lives that are, in and of themselves, just day-to-day occurrences. The real poison is in the tendency to interpret, which comes forward and attaches meaning to those expressions. And such interpretation is always about dwelling on the realm of the personal:

"You didn't do well enough on this one."

"They were laughing at you."

"They excluded you again."

"This is the second year in a row that their Christmas card was a reused one that had someone else's name erased and written over!"

This tendency to take things personally will make you go for all the things that hurt, because that is your poison. It is especially good at creating imagined grievances. So just observe. And as you observe, you may even tell the story. You are aware of the story being told, but you don't get pulled into it because there is no story in the greater space you are looking out from.

Through this awareness, you will find that a change in the orientation of your way of perceiving is beginning to occur. Soon you may begin to speak of your "ex-problems."

Trust in Life

Most people go through times in their lives when challenges seem to come from all sides—personal, professional, spiritual. In those times, it can be difficult to trust that these transitions are opportunities for tremendous growth and even awakening to occur. You cannot tell what the shape of things will be at any given juncture in life. You cannot know how it will all turn out, yet all too often we act as though we do know.

The King and His Counselor

Once there was a king, and this king had a wise counselor. Now, the king himself wasn't very wise, but he was wise enough to know that the counselor was wise. The counselor went virtually everywhere with the king, except to the bathroom—but even then he would wait outside.

It just so happened that one morning the king was getting out of bed—he was a plump chap—and while getting into his royal slippers, he slipped on the marble floor, fell on his elbow, and smashed it. He yelled out in pain, so that the whole palace could hear him, and then, even before he called for the queen or for the royal physician, he called for the counselor.

"My lord, what has befallen you?"

"Look what has happened to my arm! Why did this happen?"

The counselor looked at the broken elbow and said, "It is good, my lord—"

The king became very angry. "How dare you say such a thing? Get away from me!" He summoned the royal guards. "Guards, take him away!" They grabbed him and took him to the musty dungeon and locked the heavy door—*ka-chunk!*

The physicians bandaged the king's arm, and he spent the next week in bed. One morning he awoke feeling much better, and he could no longer bear just lying there. He was an avid horseman, so he called for the royal horses and chose his favorite white steed. He had the stable boy help him saddle up and mount, and then he was off riding in the bright morning sunshine with his broken arm held snugly to his body in a sling beneath his heavy robes.

That particular morning, the king just didn't feel like stopping, and so he rode a very long way. He rode so far, in fact, that by the afternoon, without realizing it, he had crossed the edge of his own kingdom and ended up in a strange and wild land.

There he spied a white deer and was so captivated by the rare and beautiful sight that he rode into a tree branch. He fell heavily and was making a lot of noise, moaning and groaning, calling out for help, when suddenly he found himself surrounded by a wild-looking tribe who quickly tied him up. His captors were adorned with jewelry made of human bones. It then dawned on him that he was in the land of the cannibals.

His captors had already sent a message by drum to the village—*boom, boom, boom*—meaning, *We've got a fat one!* The king was horrified as he was carried toward the village and they cheered and danced to the drums. Greeted by their jubilant families and a blazing fire, the cannibals put the king inside a hut while the wild celebrations took place outside. The king looked out a tiny window in the hut and saw them laughing while making gestures with a big skewer. He was terrified out of his wits. "Oh no, no, no, no!" he cried.

Then the moment arrived. They dragged him out of the hut toward the fire; he was screaming even more as he could see that they already had the black pepper and salt ready. At the very last moment, as they were pulling him into the fire, the sleeve of his royal robes came off, and they saw his bloody elbow in the sling. Suddenly the drums stopped. Everyone looked on in dismay. *Aw! He's imperfect. We can't sacrifice him!*

So, feeling perturbed that they had been deprived of such a juicy feast, they threw him over his horse and slapped it. The traumatized king held on for dear life with his one good arm as the horse galloped home.

A long while later, the exhausted king found himself back in his own kingdom at the gates of the palace. The guards ran over and helped him off the horse. "What happened, your majesty? Your robes are torn, and you look like you've been through an ordeal!"

Back in his room he collapsed under the impact of this close brush with death. Then, as he began to reflect about how lucky he was to have had a broken elbow, he remembered the counselor's words: "This is good, my lord."

The king immediately hurried to the dungeon. *"My poor counselor. He's been in jail for a week! I must see him."* In the dungeon, the counselor was just sitting there calmly.

"Oh, my counselor, what have I done?"

The counselor stood up. "Oh, your majesty, what is the problem?"

Then the king told the story of his capture and ended by saying, "You are indeed my best counselor. A week ago, you, in your wisdom, could somehow tell that breaking my arm was good, but I locked you up for it. I'm so sorry. How can I make amends?"

The counselor responded, "It is good, my lord."

"How can being locked up for a week be good?" said the king.

"Well, my lord, you have been wanting to go on a long ride for some time, and I always go everywhere with you. The cannibals would have captured us both, and when they saw that they couldn't sacrifice you, they would have sacrificed me. So it was good for me to be here."

The point of this story is that you never know how things are going to turn out. Sometimes we jump to premature conclusions, judging things to have gone badly. But if you just keep quiet and trust in life—but don't wait—you will come to see that the quieter you are, the more you are able to see things as they really are, and so your heart will be filled with gratitude for that wisdom.

The mind is always acting prematurely and is quick to pass judgment; therefore, it is always misinterpreting things. But what may seem like life being challenging may really open up the possibility for your mind to see in another way, to perceive the beauty that you might not have appreciated at this subtler level of consciousness had you remained in a better situation. These quakes can actually be great motivators, great facilitators, for a deeper understanding of your own nature. All of this is part of life. It's natural that things go wrong sometimes—they go wrong so that they can go right.

Welcome the Lion on Your Path

Papaji used to tell the story of a young woman who was about to get married. The wedding was to be held the very next day, and she was in the full thrill of the preparations. Now this young woman lived in the forest; so she started to walk to the nearby town with the list of final appointments with the baker, florist, dressmaker, and priest. It was springtime, so everything was in bloom. She was absolutely brimming with the joy of life, skipping through the forest, absorbed in visions of her beloved, the coming marriage, children and grandchildren, and how blissful her future would be surrounded by those who love her.

Then suddenly a lion, a hungry lion, appeared right in front of her on the path. He was so close that she could feel and smell his breath. In that instant, the baker—gone! Dressmaker—gone! Florist and priest—gone! Even her beloved, the light of her life—completely gone! At that moment she was absolutely alone: no time, no future, no intention, no past, no identity.

The master says: welcome the lion on your path! Until you do, you will always be planning a tomorrow you don't have and a next week that nobody can promise you, and your mind will reverberate with the noise of otherness and changefulness.

We have all acquired the habits of projecting into the future and clinging to the past. We are full of the claustrophobic noise of identity, intention, promise and fantasy, future and past. What will strip you back to that place before and beyond time and intention? How far from there are you right now? What's left for you to do, what unfinished business, before you can simply be left as the pressure-less Self? Remember, the mind is not going to just take a holiday. What will bring you back into this instant? When will you have a moment to be just you, not carrying a message for tomorrow, but a moment for your own Self?

WELCOME THE LION ON YOUR PATH! UNTIL YOU DO, YOU WILL ALWAYS BE PLANNING A TOMORROW YOU DON'T HAVE AND A NEXT WEEK THAT NOBODY CAN PROMISE YOU.

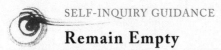

Remain Empty

There is something that is not in the next moment and not in the past moment. You don't need to look anywhere to find it. Your very search to find it is already arising in it.

We have been missing the obvious,
but don't seek help from your mind to find it.
Simply leave all these engagements aside.
Leave aside all intentions, dates, appointments,
speculation, promises, and aspiration.
Leave aside past, and don't touch *what's next*.
Leave even the concept of *now*.
Leave everything aside for a moment.
Don't touch anything—sensations, thoughts, feelings,
memories, expectations—leave everything aside.
Discard all interest in these and remain empty.

You are just here.
Feel the sense *I am here*.

Now, drop *here*,
drop *am*,
drop *I*.

Not touching anything, not even 'I,'
what remains?

What size are you here? What shape?
Can this fade?

Can you come to the edge of your Self,
beyond which you are not?

Something remains that cannot be set apart.
It is free of quality and immutable.
This is the Self of all.

I Once Believed

I cannot accept people's versions and visions of themselves—they are simply not true! For this reason, I am able to serve humanity. I know every single being because I know the state of the one who dwells inside to be perfect and holy. I see only the Self; but when people speak, something else emerges. I look in people's eyes and let them speak, and I wait for them to say, "Aha, it is all nothing!"

"Last night I saw an angel, but it was . . . nothing."

"Yesterday I thought I was going to die, but it turned out to be . . . nothing."

"I had an experience! It was so amazingly . . . nothing."

"I want to be free from . . . nothing."

"I have to tell you about such-and-such because something is tightening up around . . . nothing."

"I was sitting in a cave and unexpectedly . . . nothing."

"What are you speaking about anyway? It's clear! It's . . . nothing."

One day you will regard this body and this personality as nothing, nothing, nothing.

If the story is chopped away, what remains as *you*?

As you grow accustomed to giving attention to that space of awareness within yourself, the past will gradually loosen its grip, and you will feel much brighter and more present.

Some rare beings discover the immensity of awareness to be so profound that it erases all suffering—and the sufferer, too. You must discover the value of awareness by observing more and identifying less. Observe even the tendency to identify. Observe it, but don't connect up, don't log in to your observations.

There will come a time when you will say:

I once believed everyone had to like me
and that I needed people's respect
in order to be valid as a human being,
but now I see it's just not so.

I once believed I had to be
the very best person I could be in order to be free,
but now I see my striving ended up causing a lot of trouble.

I once believed
I could only turn my attention to spirituality
once I was satisfied that I had made
my mark upon the world,
but now I see this was a very limiting way
of looking at life.

I once believed it was up to someone else
to make me happy;
now I know I can be happy with other beings,
but I cannot depend on others
to be the source of my happiness.

I once believed
I could always rely upon my friends in times of need,
but now I see that help may come
from unexpected quarters and in mysterious ways.

I once believed I was not worthy,
but now I see such a thought
was merely self-defeating nonsense.

I once believed I had to practice more,
meditate longer, be more sincere,
but now I see that life need not be so strenuous.

I once believed I was not ready for Truth,
but now I see I am already that Truth.

I once believed so many things that are not true,
but now I see they were imagination,
and all along I was simply missing my true Self.

I once believed so many things
that were just not true.
Now I realize that nothing obstructs
the freedom that I am.

Now I am here.
This life is for freedom. I choose that.
This day, this hour, this moment is for freedom.

Initially, the more you reenter your space of freedom,
the more the seeds of the mind may grow
into aggressive weeds that are demanding,
almost commanding, attention.
Although the mind's whole show
is only a passing phenomenon,
you may feel that these special effects are real,
even if they are merely the thousandth repetition
of old psychological material.

The ways of the mind are ancient, but the Self is timeless.
So don't get entangled in the mind's thicket,
and you won't lose touch
with your inner harmony and Self-focus.

Go All the Way

MANY BEINGS WITH the urge for true freedom ask how to be free from the limited sense of personhood. They say, "Please help me destroy this ego that is causing so much trouble. I want to be rid of it!" However, I prefer to say "transcend the ego" rather than "destroy it." You cannot destroy a ghost, but you can realize the truth of its illusory nature, and then you will no longer be intimidated by it. For example, if you are walking in a desert, you might suddenly see a mirage: lovely gushing springs surrounded by groves of palm trees. Wow! And off you go. But you can never reach it. And it doesn't matter whether you believe in mirages or not—it happens to all travelers in the desert: they start to see mirages. Even after you know it's not real, it still appears on the horizon, right in front of your eyes. You cannot destroy a mirage. You cannot stop it from appearing. But you can see it for what it is and thus come to know that it is unreal.

The ego doesn't really exist, even though, like everything else, it may *appear* to exist. "But why pick only on the ego?" you may ask. "Ego, non-ego, being, and non-being are all illusory. Isn't *everything* only an appearance in the mind and Self?" Well, yes, but as long as we believe ourselves to be the ego-mind, "everything else" takes on an intensified sense of reality.

Ultimately there is only the Supreme, Brahman, and we are ever That, which is all-encompassing. Rare indeed, however, are they who truly know this with their entire being and not just with intellectual conviction.

Everyone wants to be happy, but not everyone has the same idea of *how* to be happy. We may still feel that there are ways to be happy other than by transcending ego. We may still cherish a conviction that we can be happy and free *as* ego. Others already know that freedom is not freedom *as* ego, but freedom *from* ego.

Many people say, "I want to be free!" So, I say, okay, let's look at what exactly it is that stops you from being free. But the closer they come, the more excuses they make. People seem to like the *idea* of being free more than actually *being* free—or so they may think.

Resistance to Freedom

Once, a man came to my house to talk with me. We sat down together, and he said, "I really want to be free."

We were talking for a while, and just as we came to a beautiful, subtle point in the inquiry, he said, "Um, my throat is very dry. Can I have a glass of water?"

So I went and got him a glass of water. He drank and said, "Yes, okay. Thank you. So, where were we?"

"I was talking about your real position as the one perceiving all this. What is that awareness? From where are you observing—and as who or what?"

Then he exhaled heavily and said, "It's a little hot in here. Can I open the door to the garden a bit?"

"Ah, okay. I'll open the door to the garden. Okay, now can we look? Are you aware of—"

"Ah, just one second. Can I go to the bathroom?" he asked.

So then I said, "Listen, we don't have to do any of this at all, you know, and if you just want to go, you may go. My house is not a prison."

He said, "To tell you the truth, my mind really wants to run away because it feels something that is making it very uncomfortable."

I said, "But you can go. It won't offend me."

He insisted, "No, no. Please can we try again?" With this he made a higher choice not to go with the mind's resistance. As we sat and looked together again, his mind opened up and finally settled inside his Being.

Something inside of us has invested considerable energy into untruth. It is indeed easy to say, "I'm searching for Truth," but when we come right up to the moment of truth, that's when I'm likely to hear, "Just one moment! I'll be back in ten minutes, okay? Hold on, don't go away, I'm coming!" Such a one will not be coming back, not in ten minutes, ten hours, or ten days—and maybe not even for ten years, if at all—because something inside of them is afraid to face the Real. It is so easy to say, "I want Truth," but rare are they who abandon themselves for the sake of Truth.

The true seeker must inquire into the attitudes that underlie and motivate their approach to life and to the very search for Truth. Seize your chance, which is always now. Some say that inquiring into the nature of the Self is hard, but that's not true. The truth is that there is a part of the psychological mind that is reluctant to partake in any investigation that may expose its ultimate nonexistence.

Immerse yourself in this energy field of satsang, whereby you become more aware of a greater power that rests in, and as, Being itself. Fear may keep popping up, but you no longer surrender to that fear. Awareness of this natural space of Being makes it easier to get over the fascination with the ego. You are now able to turn your attention away from ego and to hold it inside presence itself. When attention doesn't feed the ego, the ego's power is diminished, its authority broken. But if the old fascination with the transient is constantly lurking at the periphery of your attention, it's because you still have at least a little emotional investment in it. It keeps sitting at the door waiting and whining, because it knows that, eventually, it is going to get fed.

> THE TRUE SEEKER MUST INQUIRE INTO THE ATTITUDES THAT UNDERLIE AND MOTIVATE THEIR APPROACH TO LIFE AND TO THE VERY SEARCH FOR TRUTH.

This can all be a slow process, because being with our ego is like being in a bad relationship. We want to say: "I'm finished with you! Hit the road, Jack!" but then we go off and start to think about it. *Hmmm, maybe I was being a bit hasty.* So you send a little text to the ego: "Okay, let's make another go of it."

Some people can break up with ego easily, just like breaking a cracker—finished. But for others it's like a pizza with lots of hot, gooey mozzarella—they spend time trying to separate the cheese. Gradually, we start to check the ego's Facebook page less and less often, but it takes time to really let go, because we are not quite sure yet that we are really doing the right thing. "Do I really need to let go of my attachment to the mind completely?"

But as you discover your own true Self that is imbued with love, it will be easy to let go of what is not true. It's not even that you have to drop vain pursuits. God is not asking you to give up your sweeties, your favorite treats. It's just that you start to lose interest in them. At some point it will even dawn on you that the sweeties you thought you had to surrender, you actually never had. They were just the false promises of the mind of something to gain in the future so that you could be happy and content. And so, gradually, one comes to hear the mind's call ever more distantly.

You may look at it this way: even though there are dark spots on the moon, its light is not diminished by them. In the light of your own inner reality, the shallowness of the egoic mind has lost its appeal for you. It is no longer the focus of your concern because a greater light illuminates the world.

Beyond Opening and Closing

Some people have had a taste of the Truth. A glimpse. They have opened, and it is wonderful, but then after some time, they feel a sense of closing up again. So they set a firm intention to open up for good. They come to me with this news and ask me to remove whatever obstacles are left to their total freedom.

This sense of opening and closing has been granted more importance than it really deserves. The great joy and harmony of opening and the more personal and tight sense of closing are both conditions that are observed from a deeper place. I'm constantly pointing to this witnessing because *you* are the witness. All that is seen is subject to change, including the sense of opening and closing, in-and-out-ness, coming-and-going-ness, whereas the witness is stable.

Many seekers report finding and losing the sense of freedom. This is because they are still trying to use what is, by nature, changeful as a reference for themselves. We can invest a lot of time and energy in watching the changeful, hoping that one day the beautiful manifestations will remain in place. But that's not how it works. It's not that we will come to a level of the manifest that will never change.

It's more important to discover *where* we are looking *from* and *who* or *what* we are looking *as*. Up until now, we have been so caught in the bubble of what is being seen that we have forgotten about the source of that perception. And when I say *seen*, I don't mean just in terms of images or sensory impressions, but also in terms of the effect generated on the body and the accompanying feelings—all of this is part of perception.

In reality there is no such thing as someone being able to "stay permanently" in the Self. No one has ever done it: the Buddha couldn't *do* it, neither could Christ *do* it. Rather, the Self has been recognized as what we are, and it is effortlessly and timelessly perfect, always. In truth, there is no actual "in and out" of the Self, no fluctuation—for these are seen to arise within the immutable awareness.

Don't pay so much attention to the sense of opening and closing, otherwise the mind will use this to perpetuate the feeling that you are not yet what you already are. It will argue, "If you were the Self, you wouldn't be experiencing such fluctuations!" That experience of opening and closing is still phenomenal in the light of a greater seeing, but deeper than that, one is open in a way that is nonphenomenal. We don't call it openness because it doesn't have the counterpart of closedness. It is beyond opening and closing.

When the Person Is on Its Way Out

There comes a time when it is recognized that the personal sense is appearing in presence, but the presence is greater. The sense of the individual person is still there, but it's on the way out. It's like a snake that's leaving the room: his head is in the garden, but his tail is still inside the room. Let him go out, as he's leaving anyway. He can't stay because the temperature is no longer right for snakes. In much the same way, the personal sense will still be there, but it will slowly be inching its way out the door and losing its power over you. But you are also not waiting for it to be gone. The one who is *waiting* is still an aspect of the mind.

Keep your energy and your concentration focused only on the Self, not on the personality. If you were the personal sense, you would not be able to witness the sense of personhood and its antics. The sense of personhood is unstable and inconsistent, but it is trying to find consistency. It is the one reporting on the comings and goings. But the paradox is that this one who is striving for consistency is itself inconsistent. If you want to find consistency, personhood has to go—only then is true consistency revealed. That is the trick somehow.

> We identify as the person
> who is going to receive something beautiful.
> But the beautiful is already here,
> it's just that the person is hiding it.
> This mystery is now revealed to you.
> So don't pay so much attention to identity.
> The more attention you give it, the more real it seems.
> Know that it is only you who gives reality to these occurrences;
> they have no reality in themselves.

This is why the mind needs your investment of energy and belief. Otherwise, it cannot become manifest any more than a lightbulb can glow without electricity. Through your attention, identity, interest, and belief, you supply the electricity that energizes thoughts. Once you see this, you will recognize where the real power lies. The power is always with *you*, not with the thought. For as long as this is unclear to you, thoughts will seem to have a life of their own.

Thoughts Don't Necessarily Mean Thinking

For a while, thoughts may continue to appear, but the arising of a thought does not, in itself, amount to thinking. A thought without belief has no power. But a thought *with* belief can start a war or begin to heal the pain of an entire nation.

A THOUGHT WITHOUT BELIEF HAS NO POWER.

It is your belief in thoughts, and your identification with them, that breathes life into them and can cause great pain and suffering.

Much like the actors in a play won't come on stage until the audience is seated, thoughts won't perform without you, the perceiver of them. Thoughts cannot think themselves, because thoughts are not sentient. Therefore, they cannot, by themselves, turn into thinking. For thinking to occur, thoughts need to link up with the thinker-thought, the 'I' that is interested in the play and its outcome.

The same thought that troubles you may arise in another and pass by barely noticed. No thought has any inherent meaning or power. It is you—through conditioning, habit, belief, and identification—who gives meaning to particular thoughts. Once you have become identified with a thought and are seemingly pulled into thinking, the watcher of that thought-play somehow also becomes a part of the play. However, that which knows *all* of this is not caught in the bubble of that play. In and *as* such a wider field of awareness, we are able to see even the attention being pulled into identifying with thoughts.

Stay in this space of neutrality, in this neutral place of witnessing. This is the real Self.

If I were to urge you to stop your thoughts, could you accomplish such a feat? It would be like swatting flies outdoors. The more you go after them, the more they seem to appear. We cannot place memories, worries, and other thoughts under arrest. So let the thought-flies buzz, but shift your attention toward awareness itself. Just let the thoughts play, and you stay as awareness. Compulsive thought activity will naturally begin to subside without effort. In a sense, you are no longer feeding the animals, and so they soon disappear.

Stop Feeding the Pigeons

Trafalgar Square is a famous landmark in London and one of the sights that tourists always visit. For decades it was a tradition for people to feed the thousands of pigeons that flew around the square. Vendors sold little cans of corn and took pictures of people feeding the pigeons to make a few pounds. But with all the pigeon poop building up on the ground and benches, it was becoming a filthy place. So the mayor scheduled a press conference at Trafalgar Square and declared, "As from such-and-such a date, it will be illegal to feed the pigeons. Why? Because we are a modern city, and it is not sanitary to have all this pigeon poop everywhere. We have to get rid of the pigeons, but this is a civilized country, so it is also illegal to kill them."

Then the day arrived when people stopped feeding the pigeons. After two weeks, no pigeons could be found. They were showing up in my town and other places around London where we hadn't seen any in a long time—but in Trafalgar Square, none.

If you don't feed the pigeon-thoughts, you won't have to kill them. Not feeding the pigeon-thoughts simply means keeping your attention in and as awareness itself. Withdrawing your attention from the constant stream of thoughts is not cowardly. It isn't that you're running away or that you're afraid. Rather, staying in presence is the wisest response, because without your attention going to those thoughts, they cannot proliferate or grow, and so they will subside on their own. Just stay as aware-ness—it's that simple. For some this advice seems naive or overly simplistic, but it is immensely powerful!

Without attention and identification, the bothersome thoughts of the egoic mind lose their power and become like the moon in the daytime sky—pale and insignificant—until finally, you don't notice them at all.

Don't Get Entangled in the Mind's Thicket

Giving energy to the mind is like asking someone to harass you. Once you see it—aha! The game is up. However, the psychological mind, the devious mind, the mind in its aspect of deceiver and tempter speaks with the serpent's voice. It will still try to find ways to work through your weaknesses and so gain entry to your house. It will sneak in through your blind spots.

But you are stronger, infinitely greater than the lie. And all lies flee in the face of Truth.

Now you have asked for the veil of delusion to be lifted—so be it.

Initially, the more you reenter your space of freedom, the more the seeds of the mind may grow into aggressive weeds that are demanding, almost commanding, attention. Although the mind's whole show is only a passing phenomenon, you may feel that these special effects are real, even if they are merely the thousandth repetition of old psychological material. The ways of the mind are ancient, but the Self is timeless. So don't get entangled in the mind's thicket, and you won't lose touch with your inner harmony and Self-focus. Remember: you will never be free *as* ego; freedom means freedom *from* ego.

You must remember that whatever is happening, no matter how intense, it is still only a phenomenon. It is not going to stay; it only *appears* that the current condition or situation will last forever. The effects cannot endure because they are not real. They are subject to change—and so it goes with all that is phenomenal. Pay less attention to these energies. Stay in your unitive power, which means to remain in a kind of neutrality.

My own life has me moving about among all kinds of events. Each day, so many ideas and requests come to my ears—"Can you take a look at this? Can you decide about that?" But none of it can divide me from what I am. As I naturally interact with people from and as that unitive power, everything informs my actions in the world without the need to strain to comprehend it all. I can see that the whole universe is unfolding by itself and that my body is part of that whole.

We will probably never leave our conditioning behind completely. It may remain with us on a superficial level and continue to have some small effect on us, but it will no longer be authoritative and commanding. If you have preferred mild food all your life, you won't suddenly wake up craving extra spicy curry!

This life is your chance to be in your power and in your holiness. And this is good news, because you are being freed, not bound and sentenced. You are being delivered by virtue of your own seeing and your own satsang. The force of conditioning had you hypnotized for so long, but now you are being set free from this spell. How can this spell be broken? Just follow this pointing: remain as awareness.

Freedom Is Free—But Not Cheap

After having had an experience as profound as discerning the real from the unreal, your mind may want to show off by demonstrating your discovery and taking credit for it. What better audience than a few acquaintances? But going out and engaging in chitchat or other trivial activities hemorrhages your energy. It is a sure way to fall back into delusion. You have given in to the lure of the mind, and by falling for the mind's temptation like that, you go out into the fish market again and divide yourself. Thus, the energy and fruits of that realization leave you.

There are some people I see only once each year for just an hour or two, but when I see them, I can tell that during the time we have been apart physically, they have cleared away more of the conceptual noise that had been there a year earlier. They have been quietly emptying out into nothingness. It is not your visibility that I find attractive, but rather your invisibility. Only in the absence of the personal sense is your presence revealed, and presence is radiantly beautiful. When you are presence, I see you.

Even in holy places, there are people working to make noise and to help you celebrate your own noisiness. Even if they don't mean any harm, you must avoid their company. Many who have a powerful awakening just want to keep quiet. To avoid losing energy to the usual nonsense of the personal realm, they don't want to come into contact with anyone. They know that what they have absorbed is far too precious to sprinkle about.

When you sense that you have had a chance to merge the mind deep inside its own source, that you can feel the presence of the Supreme Being in your heart, that isn't the time to go to a cafe or hang out on the Internet. Go home and sit in this oneness. Say yes to the Truth inside your heart. Take the attitude, "Rid me of ego and dissolve my mind in You, the Divine Presence. Replace me with You. I say yes, yes, yes to the True."

When you have just made such a breakthrough into real seeing, but then interact in a way that reflects your own habitual, egoic thinking, thereby squandering your treasure, it might just be that you still haven't recognized the value of what you have discovered.

The Miner and the Celestial Gem

Once upon a time, there was a man who made a meager living from mining semiprecious stones. He would go out with his donkey every day in pursuit of his livelihood. Sometimes he would go for hours on end swinging his pickax in the hot sun, chipping away at rocks with sweat running down his face. When eventually he would find a little bit of amethyst or rose quartz, he would burst out in excitement—"Oh, my God! Look at that!"—before putting the stone in his little bag.

His routine was to go chipping for a few hours in the cool of the morning and then take a break under a tree, having a piece of bread and a bit of water before returning to his arduous job for the rest of the day.

One day he was sitting under a tree, taking a break from the hot sun, when suddenly he heard *boom!* A celestial gem fell from the sky and landed right in front of him. After recovering from the initial shock, he bent down and picked it up. The sparkling gem was enormous and priceless. It was a jewel from heaven itself. He looked at it more closely and saw that it was completely transparent—crystal clear.

"Well, what is this?" he mumbled to himself. As a miner of semiprecious stones, he had never seen anything so remotely pure and clear. He mistook the celestial gem for a nice piece of glass and tied it around the neck of his donkey with a piece of string. "Ah, that's where that shiny little ornament belongs!" And so he went back to chipping away at the hillside looking for something of value.

From a distance, a man had been watching. Suspecting that the meteorite gem he had seen falling from the sky was rare and priceless, and having seen how nonchalantly the miner had treated the whole affair, he decided to pay the miner a visit. As he got closer, the glint of the gem around the donkey's neck confirmed his suspicions. He approached the man and said, "Hello, sir."

The miner looked up from his chipping and said, "Hello."

"Pardon me," the stranger went on. "I need to go to the next city for a very important appointment, but I'm very, very tired. Can I buy your donkey from you?"

The miner, not astute enough to catch on, said, "My donkey? Now why would you want to buy my old donkey?"

The clever man said, "I simply must get to town, and your donkey is the only way to get there without having to walk. I will pay you three hundred dollars for him."

The miner replied incredulously, "Three hundred dollars for that old beast!?"

"Yes. It is an important matter, and I simply must get there quickly."

"Sure! At that price, you can have him!"

So the man gave the miner his three hundred dollars and went off on the donkey, *clip-clop, clip-clop*. When he had gotten far enough away and around several bends in the road, he dismounted, took the celestial gem, and with a slap, turned the donkey back toward where the miner was. *Clip-clop, clip-clop*, it walked straight back down the road and stopped when it reached its true owner.

When the miner saw his own donkey returning, which he had just sold for such a handsome price, he exclaimed, "What strange people there are these days! They go and pay three hundred bucks for an old donkey that's barely worth a hundred, then change their minds and just let it go!? Ah, how foolish people are! I guess some people just have money to burn!"

And he went right back to chipping away at the rocks without giving the matter a further thought.

Discovering our true Self is akin to finding that priceless gem, but we may not value it because we are still too invested in the familiar distractions of the world. We are too easily tempted by the ego-mind and its idle promises. All too often I hear reports from those who recognize the spaciousness of the Self and the joy of Being, but who then quickly go out into the red-light district of the mind and squander it all. Then they come back, saying, "I feel a bit dull. Maybe I really should have given myself more of a chance to marinate in those insights." One has to take this opportunity seriously, because freedom is free but not cheap.

You have everything: you are alive and have an urge that impels you toward the Truth. Something inside of you is calling out for freedom, and you want to harken to that call. But something also divides your attention and keeps you back. You must slay that dragon of deceit. You have the power to prevail—not as a powerless little person, but as the all-encompassing oneness. You have great power, most of which you have not yet even begun to use. But you are here to recognize and reclaim that power. Bring your entire Being to the table of Truth.

The Ultimate Truth Is Not an Experience

Spiritual seekers often ask me to comment on blissful, cathartic, or other impactful experiences they have had since dedicating themselves to Truth. They ask me to help them clarify what the real significance of such experiences might be. Perhaps for some days or weeks, they have been moving in a deep sense of oneness with everything, and now they wish to know if that means that they have "got it" and can now share their discovery with others.

Also, as people go more deeply into their inquiry or along their spiritual path, some gifts and talents may manifest or become more pronounced. For example, you hug someone and all of a sudden they say, "Thank you for healing my shoulder!" And you start to think, "Wow! I am blessed with the gift of healing hands. I am meant to become a healer." Or perhaps you suddenly find that you can sing like an angel, and there is a temptation to make much of this. But if this happens, you must remember that your choice was for freedom; it was not to become a famous singer. Of course, if you sing, by all means sing, but sing just for the joy of it. Then, if more comes of it, that is fine. Just don't place your singing career on the front page of consciousness.

> WHATEVER YOU ARE EXPERIENCING, NO MATTER HOW BEAUTIFUL OR PROFOUND, IT IS ALL STILL PHENOMENAL.

Whatever you are experiencing, no matter how beautiful or profound, it is all still phenomenal. It is not uncommon that many beautiful things may happen as you become empty of the sense of personal identity, but it's not like a bag of tricks or passing a series of milestones. When such things arise, you must remind yourself: "I didn't embark on a spiritual path to develop special qualities. I am going for freedom!" Go all the way, and don't settle for anything less.

Temptations of a Great Yogini

A great yogini was meditating in a mountain cave, intent upon discovering her true nature. While in this deep contemplation, suddenly the most beautiful, iridescent colors appeared in front of her. The colors were shimmering and far more vivid than any artist could ever paint; no flowers on Earth could be as delicate, detailed, and radiant as these living, changing shapes. She felt, *This is extraordinary, amazing, and so beautiful.* But then an inner voice came: *This can't be what* I am, *because I am here perceiving these colors.* And then the colorful shapes quickly danced away and disappeared.

After a short while, she heard the most beautiful music—so melodious, soulful, and rhythmic, so absolutely delightful. Who had composed it? She was deeply moved. *No composer on Earth could have composed this!* But then a deeper awareness reminded her: *It may be beautiful, but it cannot be what* I am, *because I am here to hear it*—and then the music faded.

Next, luminous heavenly beings appeared and came floating toward her to embrace her. She felt their warmth, their divinity, and their innocence, but then she realized: *These beings may be celestial, but they cannot be my goal because I am here to see them.* And so they vanished. And finally her mind became totally absorbed in the heart.

In the process of discovering one's true nature, one may indeed experience many beautiful states brought on by the growing sense of oneness and wonder. We may have some true experiences, which are necessary for the consciousness at that time, but the ultimate Truth is not an experience. We should be careful about coming to premature conclusions, for the mind loves to claim, "This is it! I've done it! Hallelujah!" The mind would love you to run out and tell your friends.

Then, should that experience pass—which is inevitable in the realm of experience, the realm of time and change—the mind will try to use this as proof that you still have a long way to go on your spiritual journey. Something deeper knows that this is just another voice; both the one claiming the experience and the one interpreting it are not real. This understanding is grounded in a deeper awareness that wants nothing at all.

The sense of arrival based on a set of sensations is still the person. It is ever *trying* to get to Truth and gets carried away in the idea of, *Wow! What has just happened? It was so beautiful. It must mean that I have arrived.* You may be grateful for beautiful states that arise and the insights they offer, but don't become attached to anything that comes and goes, and don't let any object distract you from understanding that *you* are the subject in which even these beautiful states arise.

The Self is not a state. I may sometimes refer to it as a stateless state or a feelingless feeling, but it is infinitely broader than any state or feeling. It is a common misconception to take a particular feeling to be the Truth. If the Truth were a state or if it required one to feel a certain way, this would be to limit the limitless. People often ask me how they can become stabilized in the Self. Just be. Don't think about how you can *become* this, for it is not attained by the use of any technique. It is the recognition of what is timelessly present.

You are already here.

This is a mighty existence,
and the ultimate Truth is in each and every one of us.
If we can say that life has a purpose,
it is that of unveiling this Truth
so as to win oneself back from the state of hypnosis
and awaken to the Real.

In satsang, in this climate of spiritual grace,
the Buddha nature, the Christ light, or consciousness
is revealed and set free
from the illusory imprisonment
of psychological identity.

May our lives be the very evidence of Truth.

Grace Is on Your Side

IT CAN SOMETIMES seem like the mind tries very hard to stop you from recognizing the light of pure consciousness that is already shining as your Self. The mind has made a strong and determined vow: "This one shall not get through!" So you can be sure that it is going to look for any little weakness it can find to stop you from entering that place of oneness that has been called *nirvana*.

A Twig Away from Nirvana

There once was a man who was beautifully dispassionate, kind, and detached from everything. He was so empty of himself, so quiet, that he was almost invisible. He was married and had children whom he loved dearly, but he was not attached to them either. Nothing seemed to bother him. Even when he came home from work early one day and walked in on his wife having a great time in bed with the milkman, he simply said, "Oh, hello. How are you, dear? I see that you have a friend over. Enjoy, enjoy! Don't let me interrupt you. Shall I perhaps make you both a cup of tea?"

He used to say to his wife, "Whatever makes you happy makes me happy." But his wife only thought, *What kind of man is this? Most men who walk in on their wives become furious or at least feel betrayed, but this one is not worried about anything at all!* And so, uncomprehending and unappreciative of his true detachment, she said to him, "You are a good person, but I need a real man." And so she left him.

Then his children confronted him: "What kind of father are you anyway? Everyone knows this scandalous story and your strange reaction. You're a terrible father! The milkman would be a better dad than you!" He responded in his clear, peaceful way, "Oh yes, you're probably quite right. I'm not such a good father." Even more infuriated by his continued detachment, his children said, "We don't want to have anything to do with you!" He was now left quite alone, but as he was unattached to any particular outcome, he was unperturbed by his family's judgments.

So he went on his way, and after a while he found himself in a monastery. He was deeply content with his work there, which was to clean and rake the sand of the Zen garden into beautiful circles. He did this with great care, and afterward, he would sit on a rock in meditation. But he didn't have to meditate because he was meditation itself, completely absorbed in his Being. So detached, so quiet, so empty was he that he even started to become invisible. Those walking through the Zen garden very often wouldn't notice him at all.

Now, the king of the demons heard about him and called for his best—or worst—demons. He bellowed, "It has come to my attention that a mere mortal is about to slip into nirvana. Who is responsible for this one?! You're supposed to be watching over him! How could you allow this?"

Then the demons responded, "Your majesty, we already have him under surveillance."

"Well, how could you allow him to become so transparent? He's disappeared almost entirely. We simply can't allow this!"

"But my lord, we have tried everything! We have sent every test his way. We sent the milkman to his house to seduce his wife, but he seemed completely untroubled! And then his wife and children rejected him, and he took it all in his stride. We've done everything we can think of, and we just cannot get him. We don't know what else to do!"

The king of the demons said, "He's still a mortal creature. There must be *something* you can find that will distract him. We cannot afford for even one single human being to escape. You know how much trouble they cause when that happens! Now, go and pay close attention to him! Everyone has a weakness, and we must find his!"

"Yes, your majesty," they bowed, and off they went.

One day our detached monk had raked the gardens beautifully, and he was sitting on his favorite rock. He took a deep breath and was soon in deep meditation.

The demons arrived and took their stations all around him, paying very close attention to his every move. But he simply sat there, almost invisible, so deeply immersed was he in his meditation. At one point, the demon sitting closest to him even started going into meditation. Another demon had to shake him and said, "Hey! Don't get so close!" and he quickly moved away to a safer distance.

The demons were there for hours, just watching and waiting. Then a mighty wind started to blow through the hills and over the garden, shaking the big banyan tree that shaded it. Many leaves began to fly about, and one twig fell right on the part of the garden that the monk had so carefully raked. Now the leaves quickly blew away, but that one twig was just sitting there in the immaculate Zen garden. Immediately, the monk opened one eye to see what had happened and quickly climbed down from the rock to remove the offending twig. He threw it away irritably, and then oh-so-carefully smoothed the sand before resuming his lotus posture. All the demons looked at each other with sly grins and went, "Ahaaa!"

The demons started to shake the tree so hard that twigs and leaves were falling everywhere. Then they danced on the sand, scattering it all over. The monk, totally flustered and confused, yelled and ran about trying to fix the impossible mess. He was so deeply disturbed that he lost his invisibility and even turned bright green. And that is how the demons blocked our monk from nirvana, earning them the king's favor and a hero's welcome when they returned to the land of the demons.

What is your twig? Meaning: what will bring up powerful distractions for you?

Now hearing this you may think, *Oh, my God, this is terrible! I will have to be* so *unattached and also so vigilant. I will always need to be sweeping my inner house.* But this is only the case if you insist on being a person. As soon as it becomes clear that the person itself is phenomenal, twig or no twig, it doesn't matter to you. You're not fighting personal battles anymore.

However, this doesn't mean that powerful mind attacks will not come, sometimes even without an apparent twig or trigger. Nor does it mean that such attacks mean anything in particular. If such a storm should arise, you must bring it into the inquiry. Don't so much ask what the trigger is; rather, ask *for whom* does it matter? Who is the one who is bothered? Who still carries some identity? And be grateful for the opportunity to inquire, for the opportunity to see where the ego is still hiding.

Although this monk was almost completely free, there was still some residual attachment at play. So there was the need for that twig to fall on his garden in order to expose why he was still not completely free. The need to look in this way will be there for as long as we continue to identify personally, but don't ask when the need for inquiry will end. As one deepens in understanding, self-inquiry becomes a joy and often arises spontaneously. It also does not end in the way that the mind would like—with one reaching some final destination.

DON'T SO MUCH ASK WHAT THE TRIGGER IS; RATHER, ASK *FOR WHOM* DOES IT MATTER?

The inquiry is finished when there is no one left to inquire.

As you are beginning to live in the realm of beingness, of pure presence—or when you have at least recognized and acknowledged this reality—your daily functions are increasingly taking place in presence, not personhood. Sometimes the person is like a little shadow that comes in that you know will soon pass. If you don't give personhood so much attention, you're not walking around fretting, "I've got to get rid of this person!" That kind of self-recrimination would again be something personal. The worn-out repertoire of the mind is seen clearly and as nothing at all.

Ignoring thought is very powerful, but be careful not to become an "ignorer." Don't pick up any identity. Simply ignore thoughts! Just stay empty. This is an easy and direct way. The more difficult way is to be like this monk, who is detached from just about everything but still attached to something.

For some beings, this time of refinement is like reversing a glove: the hand is out, but the tips of the glove's fingers are still stuck, and you have to squeeze a little to get them out. Or, like a snake shedding its skin: the whole skin has been pulled away except for the last bit, which is still stuck and trailing behind him. He has to find two branches that have grown very close together and squeeze through them to pull off that last bit so the whole thing can fall away. Sometimes a spiritual practice can feel like it is serving the same purpose as those branches. You may have left so many things behind, but there is still this one sticking point that seems hard to get rid of.

For a while, consciousness wears the label of "seeker," and the seeker's goal is to come to presence, the unmixed Being. When one sees that the seeker itself is phenomenal, one is in the realm of presence, and presence is not a person. Presence does not subscribe to any particular religion, and it does not require maintenance through the performance of spiritual practices. From this place of presence, I may point you to a deeper reality yet—that even this one who is so determined to find those two branches in order to shed that old skin is itself phenomenal and not ultimately real. So, don't assign so much importance to the one who is shedding its skin.

You can be aware of your triggers, shortcomings, and engrained habits, but when you discover that it is *all* seen, including the involved witness, you need not work on this one anymore.

Once this is grasped, be careful. It is right at this moment that arrogance may come: "Yeah! I've done it!" And so the person-poison slips back in. But in your earnestness, sincerity, and dedication to Truth, something is there walking with you, protecting your way. You may not see it visibly, but grace is on your side. It is always here.

This is a mighty existence, and the ultimate Truth is in each and every one of us. If we can say that life has a purpose, it is that of unveiling this Truth so as to win oneself back from the state of hypnosis and awaken to the Real. In satsang, in this climate of spiritual grace, the Buddha nature, the Christ light, or consciousness is revealed and set free from the illusory imprisonment of psychological identity.

May our lives be the very evidence of Truth.

Backlash of the Ego

It seems that when someone turns their attention toward freedom by questioning their localized or conditioned identity, serious resistance emerges from inside. It could be described as a backlash from the ego. Previously, nothing, not even setbacks or losses, could really shake us so deeply. We would just go on with the usual play of acting, reacting, and interacting, all with the permission of the ego. But now that we have chosen freedom, stiff resistance is likely to be felt.

Never does the ego make itself more apparent than when you are really onto something and things move beyond the questioning and evaluating stage, so that you are diving deeply into your own Self-discovery, entering into the very heart of Truth. It is especially at such auspicious moments that forces are at play, both internally and externally, that can sabotage your freedom by keeping your attention fixated only on your body-mind existence. It thus keeps you locked into a mind-set that would seem to block any real advancement toward authentic Self-discovery.

Where does the strong pushback come from? It comes from our conditioning, our own little gremlins with whom we have been walking hand-in-hand, all the while thinking of them as harmless, believing they are our friends, our support in life, and even who we are. When we recognize that we are independent of all of our own stuff, it may dawn on us that this conditioned one is not really who we are. We acknowledge that we have some connection with it because it is homegrown, but we understand that it is not our essential Being.

It seems that, often, as soon as we recognize our essential Being, these forces bubble up to the surface. And they are not soap bubbles, not friendly forces, not happy vibes. So you may find that you start screaming at people, you can't sleep, you're having nightmares, or you're sweating profusely in bed.

All seekers—not just followers of Advaita, but seekers in all disciplines—will understand what I am talking about here, because this topic is universal. It doesn't matter what religion you identify with—if an authentic search is emerging in you, it's ultimately going to come to a fight.

And what is that fight all about, anyway?

The fight is between the tendency to remain just as a person and the pull of liberation that feels like it is the call of the unknown.

When freedom beckons, it may feel like you are being drawn into some black hole and getting swallowed up so that you will never be able to find the little 'you' again—or at least that is how the mind portrays it.

These internal forces will warn you that liberation is the biggest risk you could ever take—like skydiving without a parachute—because it amounts to the ultimate dissolution of the ego.

Paradoxically, you are only coming back to what you can never *not* be but have been unconscious of up until now. You are not going to become something else; you are going to *stop* becoming something else. You are just going to stop *becoming* and rest in your Being—and that's where the fight comes in.

But facing down these hostile forces is not like mobilizing to go out and fight an enemy. No, your fight is an epic internal struggle against egoic conditioning and the idea you have of who you are. Your self-portrait is fighting against its own painter; but ultimately, the Real isn't participating in any fight. The fight is just taking place in a dream, and the fighter is also part of the dream. But the fighter has to win this fight, and only then will the fighter merge with what it really is—that which isn't engaged in a fight. That is how the game is played.

VERY OFTEN, TREMENDOUS RESISTANCE WILL ARISE RIGHT WHEN YOU COME TO SOME DEFINING MOMENT IN YOUR LIFE.

In order to help you, I want to share this fundamental pointing: very often, tremendous resistance will arise right when you come to some defining moment in your life. It will raise its ugly head right when you stand a real chance of breaking the hold of identity and the limitations of your mind-set.

How will you stand up in the face of that resistance? You must not give into your mind's tyranny. Psychological resistance is going to come up. I want you to interpret it correctly—as a purgative rather than as a failure; don't try to face it down with a kind of paranoid vigilance: "How dare you! You come any further, and you'll see who's boss!"

Indeed, what good would such posturing do when the actual situation is more like this: Life, in the form of your psychological mind, already has your nuts firmly in hand, so that whenever you approach liberation, it squeezes them, and you quickly apologize, "Okay, okay! We won't go there! Sorry for all that searching for freedom! I've now come to realize that liberation is really not for me, not in this lifetime anyway!" Say something like this and the psychological mind will let you go, and your life will be just okay.

And that is how most people's lives are: *just okay*.

But I am telling you that you are not here just to survive life—no one is!

You are life itself, and, at the same time, you are the witness of life. Let your attitude be one that helps you recognize this. You have the innate power to discern that a presence is arising within you that is not the mind.

The Divine is giving you a kiss from within.

And even a lightly blown kiss from God will be enough to stir you into embarking upon the search for freedom.

That kiss will set your heart on fire!

Now, if you are telling me that you have not felt the touch of that kiss, then fine, maybe freedom isn't for you, so carry on.

But even a wink from God will kindle the flame of this fire that we all need so badly.

When the blaze draws near and you start to feel the heat, know that it's not the kind of flame you cook your curry on.

Rather, this is a fire that one steps into. I say, step into this fire of Self-discovery. This fire will not burn you. It will burn only what you are *not*.

I am encouraging you to take this step into the divine fire, but I am also alerting you to the likelihood that the forces of the psychological mind will snap right back against you. Fear, desire, attachment, aspiration, transcendence, love, and hatred: all of these are part of the human story. But we also have the potential to transcend all these.

Transcendence means realizing your innate divinity, but it's not easy.

Why not? Because it's far too simple for the human mind.

Why? Because you *are* already That.

We have to imagine everything else, but your true Self is not imagination.

You may have to create and construct everything else, but you can't create the Self because it is already here.

We human beings are addicted to imagination, projection, and judgment. We may call the moment that our identification with the body and the personality came online the fall from grace. But it wasn't truly a mistake, because we were *intended* to fall. You were intended to experience the mechanism of the human instrument and to taste diversity, because all of it is divine.

You must know that you were not born to remain stuck in your self-portrait, but to awaken to your original Being. However, as soon as we became identified as persons, it is as though the narcotics of existence had been infused into the arteries of the beingness, and we started believing in that kick. It's a bit like the way that someone who drinks and speaks under the influence of alcohol "talks alcohol." Or how someone who smokes a spliff will have a different vibe yet again. Everything has its effect, and if you take it, you speak through it, and it speaks through you. And so it is that once we kick the habit of living in the self-portrait, we, as the original Being, are blissful, and bliss speaks through us.

So what is this natural high, and what is its effect?

It is that which is not dependent upon anything else.

It is just *you* as you are, not 'you' as your dreams and fascinations would have you be.

Just That, as it is.

That is what we are here to find out.

That is what's on offer here: the opportunity to look inward and find *That* as your very own Being.

The Guidance of a Master

As long as we remain in the state of being independent persons and believe, *This is me; this is my body; this is my life; I am doing my own thing; I meditate; I'm Christian; I'm Jewish, etc.*, it is helpful to find a guide who has already traveled down that path to freedom, one who knows all the pitfalls and can take us the most direct way home. Although we can refer to our spiritual endeavors as a path or a journey, I am referring to the most direct way to the *recognition* of your own true Self, as opposed to the most direct way to travel. In order to embark upon a journey, one must be trying to get somewhere other than where one already is.

THE MASTER WASTES NO TIME IN CUTTING AWAY NOT MERELY THE POTENTIAL BUT ALSO THE CAPACITY OF ABIDING ANYWHERE ELSE EXCEPT IN THE HEART.

If I were to accept the idea of a journey, it would only be the journey to get your mind or attention back to the source, which is always right here. If you were to really feel that there is still some distance to cover to be who you are, what vehicle would you need in order to come home to your own Self or heart? Is there really any distance at all between you and your heart, except for the distance of a mere thought? Ideas of such separation are nonsense that we have embraced as true—but at what cost? The master wastes no time in cutting away not merely the potential but also the capacity of abiding anywhere else except in the heart. However, most seekers still harbor a conviction that they must perform some strenuous tasks, undergo ordeals, or undertake an arduous journey. It is the master's job to discern whether the seeker's mind is fit for direct recognition of the Truth or whether further thawing away of rigid conceptual blocks is necessary.

The relationship with an authentic spiritual master enriches the mind with real understanding. In the beginning, it may not be so easy to overcome the mind's power of suggestion, but with determination, earnestness, and grace you are bound to succeed. If you persist with courage, trust, and firm faith in the master's instructions and directions, nothing will prevent you from attaining your goal. You may ask, "What if I were to become attached to the master?" Well, we've been attached to so many things in life that aren't real. If we were to become attached to one who is free of attachments, this one will break our attachments so that we become freedom itself.

The Captured Squirrel

A group of squirrels were living in the canopy of some trees and would scurry about, play with one another, and forage for nuts, as squirrels love to do. One of these squirrels began letting people get close enough to toss him nuts, even sometimes letting them feed him right from their hands.

One morning, a man came to the park early and started throwing a few nuts about. Sure enough, the tame squirrel came down to eat them, getting closer and closer until he was eating out of the man's hand. Suddenly the crafty man grabbed the unsuspecting squirrel by the scruff of the neck. The squirrel thrashed about in terror and fought with all its might, but it couldn't get away.

The man stuffed the squirrel into a canvas bag and took him to his house, where there was a small garden and some trees. There he opened the bag and quickly secured a cord around the squirrel's neck. The cord was a few yards long, and the end was tied to a brick. The squirrel fought and fought to get away, but he couldn't escape.

Time passed, the seasons changed, and the squirrel remained imprisoned in the man's backyard. The squirrel came to recognize the back door squeaking open as the sign that his captor was home from work and would soon feed him his ration of nuts. The man also brought the squirrel water and stroked its back. Somehow the squirrel got used to this life. After some months, when the door opened and the captor would come out, the squirrel would just think, *Oh, here is the one who feeds me.*

Our squirrel was adjusting to his life in captivity, but next door to the squirrel lived a dog, and only a very flimsy fence separated the two yards. This dog was a Doberman—not a friendly customer—and it would charge up against the fence, slowly breaking it. That Doberman *really* wanted to eat that squirrel up. Every time he made another attempt to break down the fence, the terrified squirrel would run to the other side of the yard, dragging the brick with him. Sometimes he actually managed to climb part way up a tree, but always the weight of the brick on his neck brought him quickly back down to the ground.

This is the life that the squirrel was living month after month through the changing seasons. It was a harsh life, but still the man was feeding him regularly.

One day in the spring, the squirrel was just sitting there eating his nuts when he heard a thrashing in the canopy of the trees. He looked up and saw a whole family of squirrels running through the branches, up and down the trunk, the way that squirrels are wont to do when they are full of the joys of springtime. The captive squirrel saw those free squirrels dancing about in the full sunlight, and at that moment, a deep sadness descended upon his heart as he saw a true life of freedom unfolding above him in the canopy. He looked at the cord around his neck and the brick it was tied to and the nuts he had been fed, and he lamented, "This is not my life!" Even just seeing free squirrels stimulated a yearning for freedom and, at the same time, a deep sadness in him because he could not frolic the way that free squirrels could.

One day a wise squirrel among the group looked down and saw our squirrel tied up in the yard, looking very tired, unhealthy, and sad. She felt that they must go and save their brother. Fear overcame the captive squirrel. Normally, in the old days, there hadn't been any fear of other squirrels. But now, as they surrounded him and started gnawing away at the cord holding his neck to the brick in order to free it, he was afraid of what they might do.

At that very moment, the squirrels all became aware of the whining and barking of the Doberman who was frothing at the mouth, absolutely *mad* with desire to get through that fence and have a full lunch. He was charging against the fence, but the terrified squirrels kept working away on that cord. And then, just as the Doberman broke through the fence, the last thread snapped, and all the squirrels, including the captive, scurried up into the trees.

Now can you imagine anything happier than this squirrel? The feeling of being up there, looking down! He was jumping about in the canopy and so very happy to be free again.

The squirrel lived happily with his new friends, fully enjoying his freedom. Then the seasons changed, and the leaves fell from the trees, and the snow fell from the gray sky. And then one day the food was gone.

One winter morning, our squirrel was sitting on the end of the branch, looking very sorrowful. The wise squirrel came up behind him and bit his tail. "What are you doing?" snapped our squirrel.

The wise squirrel replied, "I can tell what's going on in your head: you are reminiscing and are nostalgic for the old days of captivity. Your mind has created a picture of someone feeding you every day, and you want to go back. This kind of thinking is what caused you to get into trouble in the first place! Give up this lowly habit! We are squirrels, and that means we are free and we find our own food."

Then the squirrel who longed for freedom, even as he feared it, remembered his true nature and shook off the fear of scarcity forever as he scampered off into the branches.

Something in our lives is like that: we are free by nature, but we have been lured into captivity by the hand that feeds us. Then we even start to fantasize that captivity is really a kind of freedom. But one day, you encounter the immortal Being, and something inside of you is touched so deeply that you feel exhilarated and are brimming with energy. You now know that such freedom is also your true nature, and you want to be free as well. It is this very yearning for freedom that opens up the opportunity for your liberation.

But as time goes on, some remnants of the mind return, and you may begin to project and fantasize about whatever it is that the mind has chosen to use to get your attention back. Again, through satsang, you are reminded to come back into your holy state. And so it is that someone comes along and points this out when you pine for captivity; that someone is even willing to bite your tail if absolutely necessary! Thus, well assisted in finding the freedom that abides in your Self, you are full of joy.

Forget about cozy captivity. Remember the brick and remember the Doberman. Don't go back to eating out of the captor's hand. That is how you came into a sense of un-freedom in the first place.

As for myself, only by being a disciple of Papaji was I able to comprehend the auspiciousness of having discovered a real spiritual master so that today you will hear me say, "To live with your head at the master's feet is to live on top of the world."

Bursting from the Cocoon

After meeting my master, Papaji, and sitting in satsang for some time, there was one intense experience during which I became very angry at him. I had written Papaji a letter that he read out loud in satsang. Up until that point, I had felt that mine was a state of loving serenity and that I was already a good way along in my spiritual development. But when I sat in front of him and he began to read my letter aloud, something began to thump in my head: *phwum! phwum! phwum!* This thumping sound climaxed into a high-pitched ringing inside my ears, and everything started to wobble. I was fuming. He had caught hold of something inside of me that I had never felt to be there before, and he wasn't letting go, while, in fact, doing nothing at all. He wasn't making it easy for me to ignore what he was pointing to, but I was not prepared to look. A huge resistance arose within me.

What followed was a sort of cutting off from my surroundings. The inner noise became so loud that I actually couldn't hear him speak. I was just looking at his mouth moving and the entire room roaring with laughter. But inside, I couldn't actually hear them; I only heard a continuous *screech!* And then I decided, in that very moment, that the time had come to get out of the *sangha* group and out of Lucknow for good. In my mind, Lucknow had become "bad-luck-now." A wave of humiliation and anger arose and came down with the crashing weight of judgments. And I said to myself: "How dare he make light of my question! And the nerve of the sangha to laugh at me like that! I must get out of here. He is not my master. He's not Ramana. Look, it's all Westerners here—the Indians don't even come!"

It was a hot day. I tried packing my bags, but my body was dripping with sweat from both the outer and inner heat. I decided to go out for a walk to get some much-needed air and found a spot under an old banyan tree in the center of Indira Nagar, but my mind was still on fire. I thought, *If I am going to leave town, I need to get moving.* I got to my feet and started to walk in the direction of home.

What came next is really indescribable. I must have walked only thirty yards or so when suddenly, unexpectedly, everything vanished—including myself. It was as if I had fallen through a hole in the universe. Time stopped. No reference for myself existed—nothing. I looked at my hands for a sense of 'me,' but they were empty. There was no memory, no flavor, nor any context for an identity, just a vastness and a sort of non-experience experience or, perhaps it could be said, a kind of feelingless feeling.

However, something was there to notice the absence of those familiar reference points. And it did not feel as if anything was lacking. Rather, I was experiencing immensity itself, an indescribable vastness without boundaries. And then, within that expansiveness, a great love toward Papaji arose. And it was only in that moment that he actually became my master inside my heart. Until then, he had been a guru, but not *my* guru.

Sometimes resistance of this magnitude may come up as anger. At other times, you might just feel disoriented because you cannot find yourself, your life, or your references. Also, some fears may present themselves by whining in your ear, "How can I continue on like this?" But all of this fear is only the stench of the mind's burp. Satsang is a powerful antidote to this agitated dream state, and it is an opportunity to come home to your own true Self.

AS TRUE UNDERSTANDING DAWNS, YOU FINALLY GET TO TASTE THE SWEET FRUITS OF THIS BRIGHT EXPANSIVE AWARENESS OF YOUR REAL NATURE.

You have been living as a caterpillar, but one with a deep inward orientation. You went inside, and then—*poof!*—suddenly you are a butterfly. But your first reaction is, "Where's my leaf? Where's my leaf?" You may even try to keep moving like a caterpillar, but now that you are flying, you find that crawling is no longer for you.

Leave such thinking about what your life is or isn't aside entirely. Don't forecast what you believe or project is going to happen. Just be present in life's unfolding. Something is still capable of carrying this body-mind experience as it has always been carried. The difference is, now you know that the life force is the animating power driving the body-mind functioning;

it is the consciousness present in the body that gives it life and, simultaneously, observes all the fluctuations dispassionately.

Now you can also understand that undue importance has been attributed to the ego and to the mind, and you can discern that Truth and love encompass everything. This is the greatness of the consciousness that we all are. So you don't have to *direct* consciousness, because human beings are not the controllers or creators of consciousness. We are the living embodiment and expression of consciousness appearing as a personal and independent doer-of-actions and thinker-of-thoughts.

Relinquishing the sense of control is a sign of your becoming more intuitive, more spontaneous, a sign that pure self-knowledge is blossoming inside you. But you are not going to learn in the traditional way—by studying books or classifying what you observe. Instead, this knowledge will spontaneously generate waves of illumination within you. You are coming into the recognition of your real place as immutable awareness. As true understanding dawns, you finally get to taste the sweet fruits of this bright expansive awareness of your real nature.

You are in a state of grace, of discovering, not of creating—so enjoy!

Fully open your mind and heart to the call of the arising presence of the Supreme.

PART II

Life in Its
Dynamic
Expression

ONE DAY, I was going to satsang and asked a friend to wait for me so we could drive together. We each have our own motorbikes, and usually we don't concern ourselves about whether we drive together or not. But on that day, after asking her to stay, it just so happened that my motorbike wouldn't start. So, because I had felt to ask her to wait, I was able to ride with her. Otherwise I would have been late for satsang.

Then she said, "Oh, Mooji, you know everything!"

"I don't know anything at all!" I said.

Things work out because there is a cosmic mind that is working like this. You come to trust it, and gradually you begin to let go of the reins of mental control and leave the driving to the cosmic mind.

Your Life Is a Discovery

Not only does the discovery of one's true nature do away with problems, but it also does away with the one who seems to *have* problems. This is a very powerful point in our search for Truth.

If you strongly identify as your personality, then this way of looking will just frustrate you. You may say, "What are you talking about? You are not even *trying* to address my problem!" I am not addressing your problem because both you and the problem are unreal! The actual problem is the false identification as a person. You are pure consciousness, pure awareness, even when you are not aware of this.

It is good news that it is not necessary to remove all the apparent problems or blockages that the 'person' experiences in order for you to realize your true nature. For one thing, if you remove one blockage, it is likely that another blockage will come to take its place. But most importantly, this idea that you have to manage your existence is still rooted in the false notion that Truth is the result of stabilizing the experiential realm. Only when we snap out of the conviction of personhood—which can happen in an instant—will our seeing arise from a higher altitude. From the place of awareness, we can see that a problem only exists for us when we accept as fact the false idea we have of ourselves as being merely a person.

Once the consciousness falls in love with the person-identity, it will only give it up when that identification is felt to be unbearable. As long as it is stuck in the state of personhood, it will invest a lot of energy addressing issues related to personal life, with very little energy left over for anything else. For some time, this personalized consciousness cannot see that there is anything else—"Just me and my life, my family and my friends, and that's it." But the parameters of personal consciousness are very claustrophobic and limited. So, eventually one has to emerge into a wider field of seeing and being.

That is not to say that one should just ignore problems in the dynamic aspect of life or feel that trying to solve them is pointless. Not at all. In fact, as long as seeming problems are arising with any vigor, one can take them into the inquiry to see where they derive their power from and to clarify one's true position. As you become clearer about your true place, you will find that problems are naturally falling away.

Your problems were not actually real to begin with—at least not in the way that you had imagined. If your problems *were* real, they would be problems for everyone, not just for you. But, in fact, they appear real only in the mind of the one who conceives of them. What may arise as a problem or worry for you is nothing at all to someone else. In turn, their problems would not bother you. When you start to see your problems from the point of view of consciousness, you're in a completely new realm. And then, what was previously felt to be so difficult is now perceived as nothing at all.

As you deepen in understanding, you may still find that you face challenges as you move about in the world. It is not that you awaken and then your dynamic life is perfect. No—somehow there is still a maturing in your dynamic expression, but the backdrop of this maturing is now that effortless perfection of unchanging awareness. You will still be addressing life, and you will continue refining your discernment and verifying your understanding. That's part of life, and it's still there. A deepening continues to take place. Superficially there may also be some play left over from old conditioning, but it's not enough to overwhelm or suffocate you. Very little energy is going to that now.

Sri Nisargadatta Maharaj says, "I allow my human nature to unfold according to its destiny—I remain as I am." It is a very beautiful attitude toward life. There is a life that belongs to our human expression that seems to just unfold, and there is no reason to be overly concerned with it. You can allow the dramas and karmas to play out, but you remain as the witnessing principle, and something will naturally respond appropriately in the moment.

Upon waking up this morning, no one knew how his or her life was going to be expressed today. Rather, we are discovering it. Yesterday you may have thought about today, but has it come out exactly as predicted? There are so many subtleties you couldn't possibly have foreseen, all the miracles in your life—like who you would be sitting with on the bus and all the people you have encountered on your way.

Let's be clear that the advice to *let life be* does not mean that you leave off functioning in life. Suppose you are on a train and notice that someone is going through your pockets. Are you just going to let it be? No! Accepting what comes and being free aren't like this. If someone is going through your pockets and you feel anger, then let the anger be. If you feel like stomping on that person's foot, then that act is also life expressing itself.

You don't need to know what to do, because things are simply arising and unfolding of their own accord. People sit around and talk about what they are going to do, but then, when the time comes, they really don't know what to do because they are out of synchronicity with their own natural expression. It's like planning to say something to people you have not yet met. Then, when you are in front of them, there is a vibration present that you are out of synchronicity with, and your carefully prepared words are dead in front of a living power. This is the nature of being caught up in our story or identity: we're not conversant with life because we are living in the past or the future.

YOUR LIFE IS A DISCOVERY RATHER THAN SOMETHING BEING MADE UP, SCRIPTED, OR CONTROLLED BY YOU.

Life doesn't need this type of planning. Some planning is needed for practical matters, of course, but the practical mind doesn't carry a psychological odor. What causes trouble for people are the compulsive psychological thoughts arising in the mind: *How should I be? What do other people think of me? Did I make the right decision?* The one who doesn't engage with such thoughts is self-centered in the proper way, not in the psychological way. This one is centered in their own heart, and so life is much fresher, more spontaneous and intuitive. Life is meant to be like this, but this doesn't mean that you are wild. You are a free being, not a wild being.

If you live spontaneously, you don't have to prepare for life. If you follow this advice, you will keep checking in and confirming that *whatever arises is only phenomenal* and that you perceive it as such. You look and see that everything is momentary as it passes by. When this is understood at a deep level, your attitude becomes, *Let it be as it is, and I shall remain as I am.* Then your attention turns away from counting, interpreting, evaluating, and judging manifestations, and you learn to rest again in your own Being. From time to time, you may ask yourself, "*Who* is the witness of all of this?" and the mind swiftly comes to rest in the heart again.

Your life is a discovery rather than something being made up, scripted, or controlled by you. Even if you could stick to a script, it would not compare to what unfolds naturally. The one who is free is just going to let life be, knowing that whatever may be, they are not going to impose a design on life—*It should be like this*—and then hold on tightly to a favorite intention. Instead, they just let it unfold.

So go forward with activity, but keep your mind rooted in your heart.

Once you discover your completeness
as unchanging awareness,
the sense of fulfillment will be greater
than you will possibly be able to express.
And you will be in a state of presence when you are alone,
as well as when you interact with others or the world.
You will no longer feel that when you do something,
somebody must come and say *thank you*.
Instead, people will come and say thank you,
and you won't even know what for!

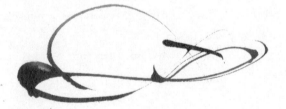

Be in the World, But Not of It

EVEN AFTER HAVING a taste of freedom through satsang or self-inquiry, you may feel that you actually *like* your identity as a person. You may feel that you are learning and evolving through it—through both the good and the bad that it brings you. You may feel there are still things you want to do, or there are still dreams you want to have fulfilled. One person came to satsang and said she was grateful for everything she received in life, including the bad things. And in looking toward the future, there were still things she wanted to accomplish, like being a great writer and singing professionally. She said she wasn't ready to give any of that up for the sake of Truth, that she still wanted to have an amazing life.

I want to be clear: I enjoy my own life, and I am certainly not promoting the idea that people ought to be unhappy in theirs. It is also true that you are evolving in your life, and it is good that you enjoy seeing the sky and meeting people. As all of this has been created in joy, why shouldn't you love it? By all means, enjoy this realm—no valid teaching would tell you not to—but don't become addicted to personality or identity.

This attitude of gratitude, even toward the seemingly bad things, is conducive to a healthy way of life. The events we call "bad" may stimulate the most profound growth, because they help us see through the murky waters of our deluded thinking so that we may dive more deeply into ourselves.

When You Want Truth *and* Worldly Success

Whatever you may refer to as the activities of the world is not in conflict with the Truth. No activity in and of itself can circumvent Truth. All that keeps duality alive is identity, desire, and the false belief in the incompatibility of spirituality with an amazing life.

The Self is already established as that space of awareness inside of us that is a non-doing place, whereby and wherein the activities of life are being seen. Therefore, an authentic search for Truth doesn't require you to assume the stance of, "Okay, I'm going to go and be the Self, so I am finished acting or doing things in life."

One person could have everything in the world and yet not be bound by anything, and another could be a monk living in the forest but be completely attached to his begging bowl. If there is a strong sense of identity constantly hankering for something, then you will always deny, avoid, or condemn whatever gets in the way of the fulfillment of your desire. You will always be postponing the discovery of Truth, and this postponement will create a strong sense of duality in you. And if you retain, maintain, and sustain this duality, then you are not going to be available for your Self. The Self may experience desires on a very superficial level, but as long as those desires matter so much to you, you will not be open to freedom.

Once you discover your completeness as unchanging awareness, the sense of fulfillment will be greater than you will possibly be able to express. And you will be in a state of presence when you are alone, as well as when you interact with others or the world. You will no longer feel that when you do something, somebody must come and say *thank you*. Instead, people will come and say thank you, and you won't even know what for! When you ask why, they may say, "I don't know, but I just feel uplifted by seeing you. You make me feel that somehow there might be a possibility for me to be free as well."

Maybe we are still thinking that spirituality and the enjoyment of one's life are mutually exclusive. If you could be the architect of your ideal life, it would not compare to the life that is unfolding naturally as perceived in a pure heart. We sometimes project an idealization of life instead of just slowing down into it and seeing the magnificence of what is already here.

> IF YOU COULD BE THE ARCHITECT OF YOUR IDEAL LIFE, IT WOULD NOT COMPARE TO THE LIFE THAT IS UNFOLDING NATURALLY AS PERCEIVED IN A PURE HEART.

Perhaps your vision of an ideal life looks like being a famous writer who is also a professional singer with a really hot guy or girl as a partner. You may indeed write or sing, but you can't determine whether you are going to be a *great* writer or singer, nor whether you would actually be happy in the way that you project.

Now, don't get me wrong, you may do fantastically well on all fronts. Why not? Realizing the Self does not cancel out an amazing life, whatever we may mean by that. And if you feel strongly to go out and get the objects of your projection, imagination, or desire, I would not advise you to suppress that urge.

We always have these contradictory forces working inside of us. Something has drawn you to Self-discovery, the search for Truth, but there is another side of you that says, "I'm not ready to be that good! I want to have fun and do all the exciting stuff in life!"

A certain resistance may come forward and project all kinds of negative images around the search for Truth: that it is an overly disciplined way to live, that it is joyless, or that it's only for people who are miserable. Quite the opposite is true: I don't think that anyone enjoys their own existence more than a sage. Such a one emanates enough joy to fill the whole world! You can do all the partying you want, but you will not be able to enjoy life the way that your sagely nature can—not just enjoying objects, but also enjoying your Self. There is no addiction or attachment involved in this enjoyment. Rather, you cannot *not* enjoy.

Sometimes I say, "Too much joy! Too much love! Too much happiness! Too much peace and harmony!" Who says something like that in the everyday world of human endeavor?

As long as we have a body, we cannot avoid experiencing. Last night I went to sleep at 3 a.m. after watching a movie and some funny videos on YouTube. Does enjoying such recreational activities stop or sidetrack me from being who I truly am? Not at all. Everything is occurring naturally. I want to dispel the fear that you are going to become a stone Buddha. I am a living being who moves about, but I am not preoccupied with what I'm going to do tomorrow.

Even if you are the type of person who always has tomorrow and next week tightly scheduled, I have nothing to criticize you for in your passion for life. Neither would I encourage you to try to suppress this energy that arises in you. But I would ask you to be open to going deeper and to pay attention to that place inside that is the source of life itself. You will not lose anything significant in doing so—except delusions. So put aside the erroneous idea that discovering your own Self means that your life will no longer be rich, full, and deep.

Although freedom is not a matter of making great sacrifices, it is true that at some key junctures in life you may have to prioritize. As I sometimes say: Freedom is free, but it's not cheap. Through self-inquiry, you have a way to expose the voice inside that still says, "I want this Truth thing, but I also really, really want that success thing too." In listening to this voice, you put freedom and success in the same category. It's almost as if they were equal. But this success is only of the ego-identity, which will continue to send up new desires because it knows you and knows what you like.

If you lend your desires such importance, then of course your attention will fly to them. You will experience a sense of agitation, of being divided, and the fear of losing what you have worked so hard to get. All these disturbances generate a kind of psychic inner noise that makes you feel agitated and that suggests you have somehow "lost your center." It is not true, but your believing that you have lost it will make it feel true.

Dreams and ambitions are not in themselves a problem. It is what they have come to mean for you that is keeping you in dreamland. Stay as the space of awareness itself and don't say that anything should or shouldn't be. Then there will come a time when you simply abide in the Self, and these projections will no longer matter to you.

Then you may write, but it will be purely for the joy of expression. You may sing from a heart overflowing, whether or not anyone is listening, and you will love *cool* as much as you now love *hot*.

There is an underlying joy in the Self. Dreams will give way to peace unbroken, love inexhaustible, and life unending.

Your Place in the World

A man who had grown up in an ashram once came to sat-sang and shared that in this spiritual environment it was easy for him to let go of the mind. But now that he had started a career as an architect, he had entered a world where the mind rules, and he found himself influenced by people's world views and the sense of needing to progress in life. He wanted to get my advice on how he could reconcile these two opposing perspectives.

The true perspective comes when you see that you are not an individual 'I' living life, but rather you are life itself being lived. You set out to go somewhere and something happens that changes your intended course. It is a feeling of such joy, such freedom, to move without the need for a determined outcome. Everything is okay. Life is more like a sketch that you are drawing rather than painting by numbers.

Some beings feel that their freedom is being compromised as soon as they go back to a more structured world that imposes demands and limitations on them. They may ask themselves, "Do I need to abandon my career in order to be fully present and free?" I say that you don't necessarily need to, not if you understand that the architect is an expression of consciousness as much as the monk is.

If it all starts to squeeze you too tightly and your spirit cannot breathe, you may come to feel in your heart that you cannot carry on anymore in the same occupation. Then fear may grab you and object: "But if you give up this career now, what are you going to do?" Don't go too far with this kind of thinking. Think like that and you may get stuck doing things you no longer really want to be doing. No one *ever* knows what they are going to do. Better to look to the One inside who doesn't think, who reveals the truth to you directly.

Sometimes life presents you with a dilemma so that you simply have to choose. You have to discern which would be the higher choice in the situation you are facing. Maybe you discover that what you have been doing is not being driven by the highest motives or aspirations; rather you remain involved in it because you think you have to do it and you have no choice. This is not the way of Truth. It is never true that we *must* remain stuck. What brought you here is guiding your life and will not abandon you to misery.

You cooperate with the world according to your own maturity. Slow down and your energies will come to harmonize with that cosmic vibration and then spread out in a very different way than the old push, push. When we push, things don't tend to work out. Even the frustration we experience when we hit a sour note and create disharmony within the cosmic vibration is grace. It's just grace on the slow-cook setting.

Maintaining control in the manner I am referring to—for example, by staying in a job too long—is a kind of paranoia, a kind of fear that if you let go, your life will fall apart. Sometimes your life needs to fall apart! But the mind laments, "Poor me—now I'm really finished!" What's finished? Only your delusions are finished.

Some people have jobs they enjoy very much, but they don't make much money at them. Then they find another job that pays more money, but they are not happy. They have no friends at work, and the boss is unkind, but they have already prioritized having money over being happy. For others, it starts to feel like their career cuts off their air supply, and it doesn't matter whether it pays a lot of money—it won't be worth it. Each person will find their way as they tread the path they have chosen.

The Self is the source of money as it is the source of everything. You must never think that spirituality means you won't have money. But, if you *were* to find yourself without money, you would find yourself with something greater than that. Some people have to discover true happiness through being broke because they had been putting more value on material possessions than on their own Being.

When these big changes began happening in my life, it all played out in Brixton, the part of London where I had grown up, had gone to school, and had been teaching art. I didn't have the luxury of going to hide in the Himalayas while I was being cooked in God's cooking pot. People were looking on, saying, "Oh, my! What's happened to him? He was a teacher, and now he's sitting around under trees all day long. At least he used to paint—now he's not even doing that."

People were really bothered by the changes in me. But something in me knew that things had to play out like this. I had to be there in my hometown. At any rate, I didn't have enough money to make a getaway, but somehow I was also fully free there, and people gradually started to leave me alone.

In the years that followed, many people from all over the world started coming to where I lived in Brixton to be in satsang with me, but no one from Brixton ever came. One day, I said to a sangha friend, "I don't know why I still spend time in this town, because no one from here ever comes to satsang.

People come from everywhere, but not from here. I guess I just don't need to be here anymore."

He said, "This is not such a bad thing, actually. At least here you are free to move about." I thought, *He's right! Very good! I can go about my neighborhood and sit in any coffee shop without anyone even noticing me, and that feels good.*

Just don't compromise the Truth that is alive inside your heart. Don't worry about how people perceive you or that they say this or that. The Supreme, your own inner guru, is there in your heart, so don't mind the outside world so much. Calmly look within and move into that unicity. Don't project tomorrow. Just move in oneness and you will see that everything is fine.

The Contented Fisherman

There was once a rich man from Mumbai who took a few days away from the hectic city life and went to a quiet village on the seaside to enjoy sun, sea, sand, and rest. As he walked along the beach, he saw a small fishing boat pulled up on the sand. A man was there, just leaning against the boat and smoking a tobacco pipe.

The businessman was intrigued and said, "Ah, hello, my good man, what are you doing here now?"

"It's a beautiful day," he replied.

"Yes, yes, a very beautiful day indeed. But what are you doing sitting here? You are a fisherman, no?"

"I am," the fisherman answered.

"But you could be out at sea on this beautiful day, catching fish, no?"

"But I have already done that earlier."

The businessman persisted, "Yes, but it's a beautiful day. You could be out at sea again. There's potentially good fishing now, no?"

"Yes, yes, and after I do that, then what?"

The man from Mumbai said, "Well, then you could make a bit more money because you could sell more fish in the village than you do now."

"Ah, and then what?"

"Well, then you could buy a bigger boat."

"And then what?"

"Well, then you could go farther out to sea, and catch more fish, bigger fish."

"Ahh, more and bigger fish; yes, yes. And then what?"

"Well, and then you would make a large sum of money."

"And after that, what?"

"Well, then you could buy a motor for your boat."

"Ahh, a motor! And then what?"

"Well, then you could go farther out to deeper waters, where you are bound to find even bigger fish. On the other hand, you could hire other fishermen to work for you."

"Ahh—and then what?"

"Then you'll have a lot more money than you have now!"

"Ah, yes, yes, yes—and then what?"

"Then you could have a nice house."

"Ahh—nice house." The fisherman nodded thoughtfully. "And then what?"

"And then you could sit back and enjoy your life."

The fisherman smiled and said, "But that's exactly what I am doing now."

Everything has to do with contentment. The less you want, the less you will find anything to be wanting. The man from Mumbai could only imagine that contentment would mean getting all these things. But the simple man says, "I am already content. I'm not tired. I don't owe anybody any money. I can sit and enjoy my little smoke, and I'm at peace."

Nothing Is a Distraction

Many societies today demand a very fast pace of life. When we move so quickly, I almost feel like there is something we don't want to allow ourselves to see. It's not a judgment. I just wonder—why do we move so fast?

THERE IS NO SUCH THING AS A DISTRACTION—IT IS US WHO GET DISTRACTED BY GIVING THINGS OUR BLIND ATTENTION.

For some people, the only way they find meaning in their lives is to do as many things as possible. Their whole days and weeks and months are filled with endless activity and distractions. Actually, there is no such thing as a distraction—it is we who get distracted by giving things our blind attention.

For those who feel that meaning comes from such endless activity, have you really taken the time to look into it before coming to such a conclusion? As long as you can't sit still long enough to contemplate the question of whether life has meaning, you won't really find out. It will all be rapid-fire like:

"What is this Truth thing?"

"Okay, it's that."

"Thank you, bye."

Boom.

If it has to be that speedy just to hold your attention, I wonder if you can really be giving these pointings to the Truth time to sink in. You need to take a little time for this introspection. In doing so, you might start to feel like a tortoise in a world full of hares. You will no longer be living your life according to the values and norms of the dominant culture where time is money, as the saying goes. And it's not easy to be out of sync with the frenetic pace of your peers.

Even when there is some free time available, immediately something comes up to get stressed out about so that you can start making plans to fill the void. Many people have internalized this attitude to such an extent that they even eat lunch standing up, as they don't want to waste time sitting down. If this sounds familiar, you are far from alone. There are so many people who try to capture time in this way, avoiding real leisure at any cost. If there were an appointment calendar out for *next year*, it would already be half full. And it's all because cultural conditioning reinforces that we are always in gear and cannot allow ourselves a single moment's rest or respite from activity.

If you have come to notice this and to recognize that you are using activity as a means of avoidance, then that is already auspicious.

Running around with such agitation is not a happy state because it's a state of avoidance of meeting your true Self. If you come to really meet your Self, you come to a space of effortless being, where everything relaxes and you have time to just *be*. Don't even start reflecting yet—just be. And then, in the silence that your Being provides itself, you notice your breath moving inside of you and slowing down a bit.

Observing Restlessness

Although it may seem that there is always something scratching about in the background like a Doberman straining at its chain, you can just look and see that distraction, haste, and restlessness are merely a play in your mind. If we were sitting together, and you were to enter into that restless state, I would notice how jittery you seemed, and we might end up having a conversation like this:

You might say, "You know, something is just itching to fly out the door and get going."

"You're aware of this, so don't identify with it. Be only the awareness," I would point out.

You might reply, "But it's very uncomfortable just to stay like this!"

"There's something in you that's like this but is not trying to stay *like this*," I would say. "It is just here. Pay attention to that."

You might protest, "But I can't do it."

"It's not to be *done*," I would clarify. "It's only to be recognized."

"Yeah, but it's very hard."

"But that's only a thought," I would reply. "Don't believe it."

I have nothing against activities or being productive, but what of your sense of self, of *who* is doing all these things? If you are inclined to being busy all the time, what I suggest is that you just stop for a moment. See what happens when you spontaneously but deliberately observe the actions and reactions that occur in your body and mind.

What happens? You can do this right now.

Follow Me Inside

Don't touch the thought, *what's next?* Leave aside anything like, "After this I'm going to do yoga and then . . ." Just get rid of the program, because *you* are not a program. Maybe it's what you *do*, but that's it. Be aware of the difference.

If I want to meet you—not professionally, not as a partner in your activities—to just meet *you*, could I? I'm not interested in your activities or intentions or in what you have done before. They are not the one I want to meet now. I do not wish to meet the doer-of-actions at all.

I want to meet the one who is behind that doer, the one who is not doing anything at all. It is a place where all the things that are being done—or are expected to be done—are observed, but it is not in the bubble of that activity at all.

Just remain in this nothingness for a little while longer
without picking up any stray thought or intention.

Is there anything wanting to come into this nothingness?
Are you waiting for anything?

This space, this place, wherever it may be,
inner or outer, it simply doesn't matter,
is not associated with any intention.
I ask you only to be aware of that.

It just is.
There is nothing you have to do here.
Just be here.

You may ask, "Does it move about? Does it have a will?"
It is ancient, and yet, it doesn't feel old.
It was the very same a thousand years ago as it is today.
It is ever smooth, ever fresh.
It is timeless—yesterday, today, and tomorrow
mean nothing to it.

Don't say to yourself, "This is just a novelty experience. I'm just trying this out for now, but Pilates class awaits me and then a hike." Let your attitude be more like, "I'll let my activities wait for a minute because I have decided to be here now."

Just stay like this.
Know that you *are* This.
This is your innermost reality.

It doesn't belong to any time frame.
It cannot be possessed by religion
or made by any human endeavor.
It is just here.

All that manifests through you
arises in it, moves about in it,
and has the sense of growing, expanding,
and enjoying in it,
but *it* remains completely untouched.

It's not a question of either/or.
It's not a matter of choice.
It is just *here*.

I sometimes say,
it is here awaiting discovery,
but it is not a waiting.

The energy of attention and belief arises from that presence, producing all the effects of time and change. Attention, habits, conditioning, and identity all come and go, and their movements are observed. Therefore, it is not *you* who comes and goes. If it were *you* who came and went, then when your thoughts fly elsewhere, you would not even be here anymore. If your attention were to drift, you would drift with it. But something is able to witness and to sense that *even though the attention is now wavering, I am not wavering.*

Be here *completely*, but not here *only*.
Do as much yoga or Tai Chi as you like;
climb as many trees
and swim across as many rivers as you please.
But no matter how far you may swim,
you cannot swim out of this endless ocean.
All worlds can only exist as appearances
in the mind of this oneness,
and no world can conquer this One.

If you know the 'I am' and you can confirm it right now, you will know the 'I am' is not in any movement; it simply *is.*

As you acclimatize to the state of presence or 'I-am-ness,' even if you begin to feel like you are visiting your stressed-out mind-set again, you will not be able to stay in that mental state for long. However, you must keep observing from a place of stillness in order to derive such benefit from your witnessing. Continue marinating in that seeing until you are thoroughly permeated by the flavor of oneness.

Too Many Choices on the Menu

While some beings are prone to restlessness and distraction, others are plagued by the tendency to doubt and second-guess every decision they make. This felt need to always weigh all the options and then to habitually doubt one's choices is a double bind. It causes trouble for many people. Such a tendency creates an inner atmosphere of haste, as well as indecision; it is felt as an uneasiness and a sense of pressure. But there are not as many important decisions to be made in life as one might think.

THE PRESSURE TO DECIDE THINGS IS MOSTLY SELF-IMPOSED FROM WITHIN OUR OWN MINDS.

The pressure to decide things is mostly self-imposed from within our own minds. It is like you are driving down a road when suddenly you see another road on the right. Although you are quite sure your turn isn't for at least another five miles, the mind says, "Are you sure this isn't your turn? If you don't make the right choice now, there's going to be a catastrophe!" Believing this voice, we enter a state of panic and feel that we have to immediately decide which direction to take. But how wise are our choices likely to be when we are in a confused state like that, when we are distracted by the noise and projections of our own minds?

I used to go to a Chinese restaurant in London that is famous for having 500 options. But you know how it is when there are just too many choices on the menu. When the waiter comes to your table, you feel overwhelmed and flustered: "Okay, okay—just one moment." So you point almost randomly to one option: "Uhhh—this one!" And I am never satisfied with my choice. Instead, I'm looking at the plates the waiters are bringing other people, thinking to myself, *Now, that dish looks good!* I didn't go to that restaurant very often.

If I go out to eat, I usually prefer to go to a certain place that is also called a restaurant but is really just a house. The woman who owns it offers only one meal option per day. No choice except the choice to stay or to go. So you ask, "Ma'am, you cook today?"

"Yeah, rice and peas."

Okay. *Boom!* That's it. Some people are happy with that, but others would never go there. They like to choose.

Who Is Choosing?

If someone is always busy deciding things, they certainly need to let go of that compulsion. But there are also people who simply cannot make a decision when making one is required. Often in spirituality, this tendency to procrastinate is excused with the idea that ultimately there is no such thing as choice because everything is predestined. Both should be brought into the inquiry: who is choosing or avoiding choices, and who is suffering from having chosen or not?

Often it is conditioning, habits, fear, and impatience that choose or prevent us from choosing. Once we understand this through direct experience, we come to see the sense of choice in a very different light.

When consciousness wants to play as an autonomous human being, it manifests a sense of choice and individuality. In the mode of individuality and personality, we love to experience. We love the sense of free will, but at the same time, we may either choose impulsively and later regret our choices, or feel a sense of confusion and uncertainty when faced with an apparent need to choose.

This idea that ultimately there is no free will is not a good teaching—it is only a good discovery. One cannot preach as a doctrine that everything is predestined and there is no choice. It is better to let people move in their sense of choice. For example, you have made the choice to read this book. That was a choice, was it not? Yes, it was a choice. Was it *absolutely* your choice? No, it was a movement that started deep down inside of yourself and was directed by the universal power to present itself, and when it reached your conscious mind, you felt, *I think I'll read this book.*

You may object: "Are you saying that if I want to do something that is not destined to happen that God is going to stop me from doing it? I don't think so! I can change my mind as often as I want. It's my choice!" The sense of personal choice is fine. If not having a sense of choice makes you feel claustrophobic, then just forget about any notion of destiny and enjoy the sense of having a choice. In that case, when making choices, it is better to feel your choices rather than to overthink them.

As we become more intuitive in approaching life, we come to see that, although it is paradoxical, what we call free will and divine will do go hand in hand; to make choices or to seemingly change your mind is also part of the play of consciousness. So don't worry about what you or others may think the right approach should be. If you feel a sense of choice, then move in your choice and make good choices if you can. But if you don't feel a sense of the need to choose, then enjoy this way of just flowing with life without favorites, preferences, biases, or judgments. If your mind is free of those energies, you will find that you're happy with anything that happens. It's not that you don't care; it's simply that you don't mind, because you're in tune with the greater harmony.

Some will mature inwardly until they come to see that actually it's neither about you making a choice nor about the Supreme choosing for you. It's all simply happening spontaneously. Does anyone switch on their senses when they wake up in the morning? No, the senses are functioning on their own. There is absolutely nothing you have to do to enable the perceiving that occurs through them. When we are established in and as the Self, we come to see that everything in life is happening spontaneously like this.

From the pure place of awareness where one sees and experiences that all is well, that we're being taken care of in everything we do, and that all is moving by itself, the concept of needing to decide things may feel irrelevant or excessive. Whatever action arises is the action of the universe. Nevertheless, for as long as the body is here, the play of choice will express itself like a voice guiding you: "No, don't turn here; we need to go there." But the sense of choice itself is felt as superficial. It's a form of expression, but it is inconsequential at a deeper level.

As for me, I am not thinking about what I should do, and yet so many decisions are laid out for me to make. Something just clearly discerns whether the matter should be decided like this or like that. Decisions are being made, but not by the mind; rather, the decision is felt. Your life will be more of a felt existence, so that you are not *thinking* your life but living it by just being. The natural state of the mind is to rest in that state of neutrality.

Keep on enjoying and trusting life and you will see where that current takes you. It's carrying you ever more deeply into a realm from which you will not want to go back into the mind. You may find that you no longer have such a passion for doing many of the things you used to do, but you will still have a sense of *I would like to do this rather than that.* But now you know that strong preferences and selectivity carry the odor of the ego's bad breath, and you will cut it out as soon as it comes up.

IF LIFE WANTS TO ANNOUNCE A DIRECTION, IT WILL PREPARE THE WAY FOR YOU.

Choosing by Letting Go

Loosening yourself from the mind's grip is not a big sacrifice. The mind has nothing to sacrifice, actually. If it were really so full of treasures, then you might hesitate, but what does the mind actually have to trade in? Mostly just arrogance and delusion, and in exchange you receive freedom!

The next time you feel intimidated by the prospect of making a choice and you don't feel anything in your heart one way or the other, just keep quiet, but without waiting for something to appear. You are going to have to bear some discomfort for a bit because something inside will not want to experience that feeling of not knowing. Something wants to go, but just sit with that uneasiness. Remain as awareness itself. Then, at some point, everything will calm down. A kind of recognition rather than a decision may enter your heart. The way forward may clearly manifest, and you simply move in a certain direction.

See What Comes

I knew a man who was an actor. He had been coming to satsang for a while and wanted to do a retreat with me. But as soon as he decided to do the retreat, a job offer suddenly came forward—something that is quite rare for many actors. So, he said to me, "I want to come on the retreat, but this is the first job offer I have had for a long time. What should I do?"

I said I didn't know. "Don't be intimidated by the prospect of having to make a decision. Perhaps things will soon become clear."

He said, "The director is calling me tomorrow at twelve o'clock. I have asked him to wait a day for my answer. My mind is torturing me. I don't know what to do. I think about everything and from every angle, but I just cannot come to a decision."

So, I told him to just forget about it and to be alone with himself. "Don't you have any other advice?" he asked.

I said, "No, no other advice. Just do this. Even if it comes down to a quarter to twelve and nothing has become clear to you, don't panic. Ten to twelve, five to twelve, nothing; one to twelve, half a minute to twelve, and still nothing. Then it will come up just like this: if the phone rings, pick it up and see what comes."

I also didn't know what was going to happen.

The next morning he called. "I sat with what you said, just being present and staying with my heart. But I didn't have to wait for twelve o'clock to arrive. After a couple of hours of just sitting with this, it became very clear inside that I am coming on the retreat. And do you know what happened? This morning my father phoned me and offered to pay for the retreat!"

Live in your heart rather than in your head. If life wants to announce a direction, it will prepare the way for you by presenting feelings in your body and mind to enable that movement to occur. And when your mind is seated in your heart, even if you should feel torn, other beings will come at precisely the right time to facilitate whatever transition needs to happen. Not only does your life become wind assisted, but you will also discover how miraculous this existence is.

Seekers in all relationships
must make Truth their priority.
You may love each other deeply,
but for each of you the first love
must always be your love for the Truth,
which is the same as being one
with your own true Self.

Establish this universal love firmly in your heart,
and other expressions of love will
naturally follow and flow.
Then your relationships will find their right place
in that orientation toward Truth.

Truth-Centered Relationships

IT IS IN the very nature of life that we associate with other beings. Relationships are also an expression of consciousness, and it is through relationships of varying kinds that we grow in our human experience. Romantic relationships in particular may unearth hidden motives and latent tendencies more easily than other relationships do. That kind of intimacy goes right down to the bottom of the pot, so we can see where our deepest insecurities and attachments lie.

Even if the ego has effectively been transcended in all other types of relationships and you are now able to enjoy them from the place of Truth, the egoic personality may still live on when it comes to intimate relationships. This is why such relationships are often experienced as being so difficult. People who are not consciously working through blockages that are brought up in their relationships just suffer through them. But some seekers highly value and make good use of these challenges. In facing such difficulties, we must simply concede, "I can see that right here is where the ego still breathes and finds its life!"

Even people who start off with a certain kind of clarity and a sense of space within themselves may quietly get pulled back into some personal drama, and that story quickly becomes the front page of consciousness. Everything is about the other again, whether it's blaming them, or placating them and blaming oneself. In this mind-storm, the Truth is forgotten.

Let me state clearly that seekers in all relationships must make Truth their priority. You may love each other deeply, but for each of you, the first love must always be your love for the Truth, which is the same as being one with your own true Self. Establish this universal love firmly in your heart, and other expressions of love will naturally follow and flow. Then your relationships will find their right place in that orientation toward Truth.

Let Love Be Rooted in Presence

Is it possible to have a relationship that is rooted in presence? I ask this because we often hold a conviction that a strong sense of personhood is needed in order to have a relationship, especially one that is passionate and rich. Is it possible to be in a relationship and yet also have the freedom and space to fully discover the Truth? Yes, it is possible. A relationship can truly flourish when you put Truth first and you are firmly established *in* and *as* that reality. Truth is broad, deep, and wise enough to invigorate and beautify every aspect of your expression.

Don't try to hold onto your partner or even onto the idea of relationship itself. The relationships of those who allow each other space are the most beautiful of all. As you are coming into your own strength, you make the best partner for the right person, because you intuitively know when space is needed for either of you. In this way, you may grow and evolve through your own Self-awareness. By having respect for each other's ways, even people of different religions, cultural backgrounds, or temperaments may find compatibility. But there must first be that underlying openness. If the relationship is not all closed up or locked in, if there is space, it can be very beautiful.

When people honor Truth, their discerning powers are sharpened, and they very quickly acknowledge what is true and discard what is untrue. In a way, they become each other's gurus. They don't put their egoic natures first. They admit their mistakes, but they don't give in simply to avoid conflict. They don't need to defend their feelings, nor do they need to make too much of them. Rather, they just uphold Truth as it arises inside their hearts. It is not difficult to love like this, and it is a beautiful way of being.

We have to be strong to live true to the ways of the heart, because very often we are afraid to disappoint the other. That fear causes people to bring very bad energies into their relationships that they may dress up in some rationale. But it isn't authentic to wear disguises like that. In the end, the charade doesn't last anyway. We just hemorrhage a lot of energy and spend many years in states that need not have been suffered.

One seeker told me she is afraid to meditate at home when her husband is around because he doesn't like it. He grumbles that she's wasting her time and taking energy away from him and the family.

I said, "You must be firm in your own Truth!"

"When my spouse is in the house," she said, "I am not free to express my heart in that way."

"You must not be a mouse in front of your spouse!" I said to her.

What kind of relationship are you going to have when you must hide in the closet to meditate, or, when praying, you can't do more than to fearfully whisper to God, "Lord, I can't speak very loudly because I'll get in trouble"? This amounts to declaring the relationship to be more important than your inner Being. And what does *that* say about your relationship?

Such a relationship will not prosper. So, stick to what you feel in your heart. If you do what is right in your heart, it cannot turn out wrong for the other—even if they end up leaving you. You may shed a few tears, but then you will discover an inner freshness again.

Sometimes people think their relationship will only work out well if they make it the highest priority in their life. I have found the opposite to be true. It is healthier to make Truth one's top priority and to stop putting the relationship on a pedestal. If the relationship is to thrive, it has to flow. Things flow when your heart and mind are one as awareness itself. If you always do everything you can just to patch things up and make sure that this or that feared event doesn't happen, that amounts to living in a state of anxiety and suffering. Even if something needs to be chopped off within the relationship, that's still in the natural flow.

Satsang purifies you and consequently the relationship. You won't continue to suffer in the name of togetherness. Instead, together you may look at the things that don't work so you can empower resolution in the space of Truth. And it can work out in a beautiful way, but without the need to create such a strong concept of *relationship*, without clinginess or trying to keep things from changing.

Relationships can always grow. As long as you are alive, there will be room for growth and variation. The dynamic manifestation of consciousness is changeful. Indeed, change is vital to that realm. However, the ego is afraid of change, so it tries to make absolute what is by nature relative, to freeze what is by nature fluid.

I have found that many people seem to have an idea of how things should be. Then, when they try to squeeze life into that shape, they undergo a very painful experience. Those who are free cannot contort themselves into such shapes in the first place. They will refuse.

In any kind of relationship, you may come to a point where you feel that a change of direction is needed, and something may guide you to communicate this insight to the other. Whether the time has arrived to end the relationship or just to take some space, you may say, "I'm going to take some time away from this relationship. We need to do this. Let's do it."

If ending it altogether is ultimately what it takes to maintain your inner integrity, then end it. It will be good for everybody involved, because when you are strong enough to stand up for what is true, and you do it—not selfishly, but rather with love and for the well-being of both people—then you also have given the other a chance to recognize the wisdom in that move and to raise their game.

Often we try things out to see what we can get away with instead of being centered in the heart. Some relationships are also very competitive. But what kind of love is it when you are competing and envious of the other's successes? A simple remedy is to honor the Truth as it is expressed inside your heart. Then you will find someone—or rediscover that same old one—and grow together beautifully. I have seen relationships that were really on their last legs until the couple discovered a togetherness in presence. They became something very beautiful, because the space had been found for transformation to occur. Somehow, though, that doesn't seem to be the norm. More often than not, we live in the name of the relationship, just putting up with things and suppressing our natural dance.

The pettiness of personhood often comes up in relationships. The psychological mind finds a way of avoiding real love by attacking the relationship, eating away at it over trivial grievances that have been given undue importance. You will find that your best guidance arises from inside. Something is always guiding you in the moment. If you go upstairs to the mind with it, trouble will come. But things work themselves out when you stay centered in and as your natural neutrality, that greater space of awareness, which is uninvolved and untroubled.

When you are becoming more established in the Truth and you perceive pettiness at play, very often life will tickle you, and you will just burst out laughing at your own nonsense. Sometimes you may see yourself arguing, but all the while it is appearing in front of you like a movie. You must be enjoying it at some level, no? You can watch this verbal Ping-Pong going on—*ping, pong, ping, pong*—and you know that you are quite apart from that. At a certain point, you laugh because it's so ridiculous that you can't keep it up.

This witnessing comes to happen spontaneously, much like a reflex. This is because your heart, your Being, is grounded in its own Self. Once you are established in the Truth, your energy is no longer invested in the restless and insecure mind state. Petty judgments lose their power. They may still come for a while, but you are able to witness their comings and goings without being deeply affected.

So, am I *for* relationships? I am for relationships in whatever form they may take: those between parents and children, husbands and wives, friends, colleagues at work, or your attitude toward the world—it's all the same. If you are centered in the heart, all your relationships will be good ones.

When One Is Melting

If you are growing in awareness and wisdom, you will be able to see clearly and support yourself and your partner in the melting into universal oneness. But what happens quite often in such partnerships is that one person may be melting into Truth while the other is just feeling that they're going to be abandoned. So fear comes upon them and squeezes them. A person trapped by insecurity will not want to go too far in surrendering into that oneness.

When there isn't sufficient grounding in the Truth, we naively imagine that our partner will effortlessly fulfill and complete our notions of love—a conceptual love that is a fantasy to gratify what we think a relationship should offer. When this is the case, relationships are likely to be tested. As romantic ideals are exposed as unrealistic, frustrations come to the surface and a struggle ensues. You start saying limply, "But all is Love. We are just meant to be together. We are One." But when we find ourselves talking like this, it isn't a good sign. At this point, your partner is likely to say, "All One? No, I am one, and you are definitely the other!"

> IF YOU ARE CENTERED IN THE HEART, ALL YOUR RELATIONSHIPS WILL BE GOOD ONES.

One woman who came up here in satsang said, "I see now that I am not real, but I'm so sad to think that my husband is not real!" Being simultaneously a devotee of Truth and in a relationship will expose some remaining blind spots in us. We tend to identify with this fearful voice that says, "Maybe I'd better not abandon myself to this oneness, because I'm going to disappear to such an extent that the very term *life partner* will become meaningless." Will you back away from freedom and Truth just because of such unfounded assumptions? It is a common fear that through the dissolution of the conditioned personality, life as you have known it will cease to have meaning. You may be asking yourself, "In such a case, what is the place of my family? How will I live in the world? What will happen to my zest for life if I have no more personality?" In truth, these aspects of life don't disappear in the way you imagine; they disappear only as causes of separation and will be discovered instead as expressions of the pure Self.

In India we have images of divine couples—Radha and Krishna, Shiva and Parvati, Sita and Rama—that tell us that the notion of relationships being incompatible with spirituality is merely a myth and that it *is* possible for a balance to be struck. But this balance isn't the person's doing. It is Truth that is guiding it.

Believing that the realization of Truth requires us to renounce our loved ones can be an excuse to stay at a safe distance from spirituality. At the other extreme, there are those who use their spiritual deepening as an excuse to avoid relationships of any kind, because they have heard that one must be free of desire. For them, having a life partner means there is some remaining desire functioning, and they question how someone in a relationship could possibly be living the ultimate realization. My response to this is: life is desire! There are pure desires, which come from consciousness itself and thus are natural.

The tenet *be free of desire* addresses selfish desires that arise from the egoic identity, which sustain a contracted, personal state of being. For example, very often in the early stages in the search for Truth, and at the very point when a real recognition of Truth is unfolding, the ego feels threatened. Gasping for air, it grabs at anything that will give it life. It's similar to the way that a drowning person will even grasp for straws floating on the water's surface. In such cases, a new relationship is clearly a distraction arising from the mind rather than a natural and spontaneous unfolding. As you mature in Truth you will be able to discern the difference and move in accordance with the greater harmony.

Abiding in the direct experience of Truth is very different from any vision of spirituality that is oblivious to the reality of human bonding. Relationships can be a pure expression of consciousness, but are you willing to take the risk of being in a relationship based on Truth?

If you are fortunate enough to be intimate with someone in this way, then you are likely to be challenged and stretched. You need to be willing to say *yes* all the way. However, for that closeness to remain, it is important to communicate openly, clearly, and effectively. Even when you have to deal with very uncomfortable subjects and differences, don't lose sight of the fact that you are always dealing with yourself. There is a say-ing: "I am not seeing the world as it really is; I am seeing the world as I am." Your partner and the world surrounding you are a reflection of your inner state. When you are free from egoic identity and the need to protect delusions, what could possibly hinder your communicating about even the most dif-ficult issues in a transparent and truthful way?

The Argument

There once was a businessman and his wife who stopped talking to each other after an especially heated argument. When they passed each other at home, they would avoid eye contact, but they still kept track of each other. They had been keeping up this silence for a few days, and neither of them was willing to break it.

Now, it just so happened that the husband had a very important business appointment in another city, and he had to wake up very early in the morning to catch his flight. The problem was that he was a deep sleeper who just could not rouse himself out of bed early, even with an alarm clock. His wife had to wake him. So he was thinking, *Oh no! If I ask her to wake me up, I'll have to talk to her.*

He was pondering how to deal with his predicament. Finally, he had a bright idea, *I will just write her a note!* He took a piece of paper and wrote: "Wake me up at 5 a.m." Then, without writing even "please" or "thank you," he put the note by the side of her bed. Feeling very pleased with himself for having come up with such a creative solution to his dilemma, he went to bed and fell asleep.

When he woke up the next morning and looked at the clock, it was already 6:30 a.m.! He was completely beside himself. Meanwhile, his wife was in the shower singing, "Oh, what a beautiful morning! Oh, what a beautiful day!" He blurted out, "Ahh! You didn't wake me up!" and was about to start a big quarrel, when he saw a note on his night table, upon which was written in big bold letters: "IT'S 5 A.M. WAKE UP!"

You can see that anything less than a genuine attempt to communicate isn't going to work. If you are able to open the channels of honest communication, then your blind spots may be revealed. You may shine a light on all these dark areas, for darkness flees in the face of light. Stay real with your partner, and you won't lose the connection. You will have a beautiful relationship that is always growing in Truth and awareness.

Move through life letting your relationship be like sketching a beautiful scene. While you are drawing it, you know there is room for growth and change. This is the way of consciousness. It's not brutal. It's not rigid. It is a very fine and subtle way into the heart.

Relating Beyond Neediness

The egoic mind always wants something from other people, but this sets us up for bad relationships. They become based on the need to be loved, the need to be embraced, the need to be intimate, the need to be together, the need to be praised, the need to be appreciated. Neediness does not make for a good relationship or for a good life.

I am sometimes asked about what may happen between two people when one partner is awakening to the Self and the other has such personal needs. Of course, each case is different, but the Self is perfectly fine in every situation. It does not get fazed. It does not have to practice any technique—it simply is. And if the needy one is open, it is wonderful for them to be in a relationship with a being who is awakening.

However, at first, the fact that one partner will no longer stand for what is untrue may seem to strain the relationship.

It's not that they have become a police officer, but they simply sense and feel things in a natural way, and that helps encourage growth. But some people aren't that interested in evolving and maturing. They just want, want, want. But when they are in a relationship with one who is awakening or awake, they are compelled to grow, or else things won't work out.

It is good to be stretched beyond our comfort zone. The mind wants to reach a plateau where everything is going to be good forever, but life is not like that. We cannot just press "pause" or "save." Something is growing, and we don't know exactly how it works, so let's leave some space for discovering. That is a better space, one that does not foster addictions.

No relationship is ever going to be perfect in the sense of perfect compatibility. It can only be perfect in that when there is an imbalance, that imbalance is recognized as necessary to stimulate the aspiration for growth. But we have to be wise enough to appreciate that; otherwise we just begin to compete with our partners.

So how may one address such an imbalance in a relationship? We cannot just take something out of a manual, put it into practice, and expect that it will work. To say how would be to limit the limitless. Every relationship is unique and will flow in accordance with the needs of that particular relationship. A relationship is a living thing, and it changes as the couple moves and grows together—and yet there must also be a strength in being independent, in being apart in a healthy way. I don't mean that a sense of otherness should be cultivated, but just that partners should be able to stand on their own two feet.

It makes for a better relationship if our hearts are open. It makes for a better mother or father; it makes for a better employee or employer; it makes things better all around. The mind may try to portray staying in your natural equanimity as flat, dull, overly serious, unfeeling, like a cardboard cutout. But this is completely contrary to the truth of the matter. You in your Buddha nature are naturally the most vibrant, the most flexible, the most open, the most alive. But you are not trying to cultivate any of these qualities, because you are not functioning on the basis of need. Everything can be there. An awakened being is still going to feel hunger and wants to satisfy it with food, but they are not deeply attached to anything.

In the same way that I may come and sit with you without preparing anything to say, so the expression of the Self and life simply unfold without an agenda. I would not want to know what's going to happen. What for? It's lovely when it's fresh! I don't want to hear *about*. I don't want to talk *about*. I *am*, and this is life—not a technique. Don't listen to anyone who is trying to teach you how to live. It is not true, for you are life itself. If your attention is turned toward observing and Self-recognition, everything else will fall into place automatically. Try it and see.

Seeing Without Distortion

In relationships, it doesn't work to just try harder. Instead, there has to be freedom, inner strength, clarity, and wisdom for a relationship to truly blossom. A relationship doesn't work based on how much you give to it. It's not a matter of payment. It doesn't work based on how much you talk about it. Such efforts usually just serve to push people away from each other, because what is really sought is intimate connection, which is far too beautiful to *try* for.

When neediness, jealousy, the fear of rejection, or any other negative energies arise in relationships, it is actually an auspicious opportunity to inquire into our true nature.

JUST AS YOU CAN'T *KEEP* A TRUE STATE, A RELATIONSHIP IS NOT SOMETHING TO BE KEPT; RATHER IT IS TO BE ENJOYED FROM YOUR FRESHNESS AND IN YOUR STRENGTH.

Know that when it comes to relationships, too much intention creates tension. Once you are free of this or any kind of neediness, you are in a natural state with no need to be approved of, no need even to be loved. And there isn't any arrogance in that freedom. Can you imagine being in a place inside of yourself where you genuinely don't *need* to be loved? It's a very quiet place in which your love becomes open, broad, beautiful, and strong.

In the context of the quest for inner freedom, at the very moment we realize the true state, many ask how they can keep it. The same tendency can play out in relationships. The internal voice that asks how you can keep your true state is also asking, *How can I keep the relationship?* Just as you can't *keep* a true state, a relationship is not something to be kept; rather it is to be enjoyed from your freshness and in your strength. Then you will find that everyone wants to be with you.

SELF-INQUIRY GUIDANCE
Facing the Suffering 'I'

When you feel overcome by neediness, possessiveness, jealousy, or any other emotions, don't suppress them or deny that they are there. Merely saying they are not real when you are experiencing them as real is not helpful. It is better to take the opportunity that the feelings present to transcend not just the thoughts and feelings but also the identity to whom they seem to belong. Going to the root identity is the one medicine to cure all problems.

Ask yourself, "Who or what is experiencing this?"
Be very honest and inward with this kind of question.
What happens in your mind
if you vividly paint the scenario you fear most?
Maybe that you will be abandoned
or forsaken for another?

Take a look at what you are afraid of
and use your imagination to push it to the extreme:
What is the worst-case scenario?
Let's say someone is leaving you.
Now you have been rejected, abandoned.
They say, "I don't want you anymore."

Let it play out in your head.
Use all your powers to bring in your worst-case scenario.
Invite it in. How does it feel?
What sensations are arising in the body?
What thoughts?

Feel what comes up,
but be present in the place from which you are looking,
while at the same time being present
with the phenomena being examined.
Don't get sucked into the story.
Just look without getting pulled in.

Identify the one who is hurt. Who has been rejected?
Is it a person? Is it an image?
Now look at the picture of hurt.
Look at the person who is rejected or injured.
And that which is looking at the rejected form,
can this one be rejected?
Who is this one who is looking?
Is it a person who is looking now?

When the worst fears are evoked,
we can see who is really suffering.
See if you can identify the suffering 'I.'
Really look to see if there is an 'I' that suffers
and if it is really you.
Isn't there a greater space of neutral observing?

Like this, you are going to completely neutralize
all these things in your life.
And you will come to recognize
that you are the awareness itself.

Stay there.

This visualization of the worst-case scenario is a valuable exercise. Any scenario of vulnerability that you cannot even allow your mind to play out is like a phantom that will haunt your life. Walking around in such a state of denial is not a good way to go through life. It saps your strength. Facing your fears cuts the power they have over you in their present ghostlike state.

What are you so afraid of? See what happens when you do this visualization. Allowing oneself to play out the worst-case scenario and facing one's fears with the intention of freeing oneself of the shadow cast by them is quite a different thing to replaying one's fears obsessively to reinforce the fear. Rather, in this exercise, one uses imagination in an intelligent way.

> THE FRUITS THAT COME FROM DISCERNING THE TRUTH ARE SO SWEET THAT JUST SEEING WILL BE SWEETER THAN ANY RELATIONSHIP.

You can do this kind of witnessing with any feeling or thought. And you will come to see what has been acting in your name and to know whether it is really you or just an image concocted by your mind. You may come to the realization that an impostor has been seated on the throne. This seeing can be experienced in a very intense way. But keep looking. Be open to seeing whatever may come up without your vision being obscured by distorting lenses, judgment, or interpretation. A feeling of peace will arise in you if you can just do this.

Seeing without distortion is a skill you will quickly develop, because the fruits that come from discerning the Truth are so sweet that just seeing will be sweeter than any relationship.

Did Someone Say Sex?

From time to time, someone in satsang will ask me about sex. Inevitably, the minds that had been drifting will snap back to attention. People who may have been leaving the room will turn right around and come back in. It is as if suddenly the room had collectively straightened up. Someone may ask about having too much sexual desire, or too little, or just want to find out what I have to say. But regardless of the question, everyone seems to be interested in the response.

How can we say there is anything wrong with sex? It is natural, no? If there were to be no more sex, then what would happen? The human race would soon be finished. Sex can be a beautiful expression when it arises out of love. Without the pleasure of sex, no one would be here on Earth, and there wouldn't be any satsang. Sex brought you here—but sex is not going to take you home.

When I was growing up, I used to hear a saying, "Men use affection to get sex, and women use sex to get affection." Now, I am not sure if this is true, but an idea persists that men and women are opposites who need each other in order to complete themselves. But if "man was made for woman and woman made for man" as the song goes, we would all be each other's answers. But somehow this does not seem to be the case. I say, instead, "Man is made for God, and woman is made for God." This takes all the trouble away, because men and women cannot completely satisfy each other in the heart. Only by realizing the Truth will we discover our inherent completeness.

If your heart is turned toward Truth, everything falls into place. Your love becomes pure, truthful, and universal; everything is included in your love. But if your focus is elsewhere, you will be plagued by the incessant cravings and projections of the egoic personality, which in fact can never be satisfied because the ego itself is always in flux, always changing. Then we have to create devices and strategies in an attempt to get what we want—so deceit and half-truths may also come into play.

Don't be on the lookout for anything particular in life, such as, "I need this much intimacy," or, "I want that much sex."

As you mature in the Truth, you begin to feel an inner peaceful-ness and stability, and your focus moves elsewhere. You will no longer give so much importance to the projections of the mind.

In some people, something needs to prove itself, and so it gets a bit edgy, thinking, *I have to perform.* If this is the case, you are already in the wrong place. It is a false appetite rather than a natural coming together. True sharing will come much more naturally, and not just as a one-night stand. Such encounters may be okay, too. If you want it, why not? But after a certain point, such casual encounters tend to just become dry and hold little appeal. If you have gone a little more deeply into your own Self and have begun to appreciate the beauty, integrity, love, and compassion that are your own nature, you will not fail to see those attributes in the other person as well.

Sex is a natural part of life, but if it is merely a craving, then you must bring this into your inquiry. The habit of gauging your sexuality based on a particular projection or on an obses-sive standard can prevent you from living fully in the present. It becomes an obstacle that keeps you from establishing mean-ingful contact, because such projections and objectification can lead to a one-sided view of men or women. They come to rep-resent only a caricature in your mind. It can be that you may continue seeing them like this for a while—so let that be. Don't suppress or repress anything. Instead, bring any compulsive ten-dencies more into your inquiry. Ask yourself, "What does my attitude toward men or women *really* mean?"

Suppose you were never to have sex again. What would *that* mean for you—or for whatever it is inside of you that has this craving?

My response to questions about sex, which is such a hot topic for so many people, is usually the same: First, find the source.

Find out who you are! This is my singularly most crucial point-ing. Who is the one who wants to possess something or someone? Who is it who wants more or less sex, feels guilty about sex, or is obsessed by it?

Just take a look, that's all I ask. And then, when this inquiry is truly followed, within this great understanding, within this great non-finding discovery, everything else can shine in its own light, and sex can happen in its own way. Sex is fine—but you must also find out who you are.

When Relationships End

When you get to know someone romantically, everything starts out nice. Usually we're in such a hurry to fall in love. But when incompatibilities eventually crop up, we may ask ourselves, "Can we go beyond all that annoys us in our partner without set-ting out to reform them? Is there a love here that is greater than the apparent incompatibility within this relationship?"

Some relationships and friendships last only a few weeks, a few months, or a few years. With others, you will walk the rest of your mortal lives on Earth together. What determines whether a relationship is meant to last? Is it just about learning to be patient and tolerant, or is it a matter of compatibility of character—that without our doing, the relationship either comes to be natural or else comes to a natural end? Sometimes factors are at play that are not immediately visible and may be the effects of untraceable influences that just won't let go, as if there were a virus inside the relationship that puts it on a countdown from the start. In a sense, there is nothing you can do about it except see God in the other and keep finding out the Truth of who you are.

Sometimes I meet beings who are desperately hanging onto a relationship. It may be because they are financially dependent, they want to avoid loneliness, or "for the sake of the children." But I wonder, is it really so noble to stay in a loveless relationship when you are spitting bolts of fire at each other or walking around pretending the other doesn't exist? And if there are children involved, do you imagine they will be happy living in the shadow of such hostility or indifference? And can *your* heart endure such a situation?

It is common in many parts of the world for people to resign themselves to making sacrifices in their lives when faced with such situations—but Truth should not be one of those sacrifices. For the most part, human beings end up needing to make painful choices because they have not been able to remain truthful in relationships. A relationship only becomes rooted in Truth when a couple uses the difficulties that arise in the relationship to transcend their engrained negative tendencies and compulsions and, as a result, come into a deeper understanding of their true nature.

If you are going through a breakup, you might feel compelled to look back with the eyes of guilt and nostalgia. You might develop a selective memory. You may think, *Maybe I could have done things differently.* But you could *not* have at that stage of your own spiritual evolution. That's just the way life has played out. Don't blame yourself for this. Know that faulting yourself and feeling guilty on top of it are tendencies that belong to the 'person,' the image you have of yourself. It does not belong to *you.* I often say it is the idea you have of yourself that suffers from other ideas it has about itself. So don't put any more energy into agonizing over the past and don't speculate about how your life is going to unfold. Send your heart's pain into the Self, and say, "I am hurting. I don't know what is to be done, but I don't want to waste my time and energy just waiting and fantasizing. I leave myself right here in Your embrace. What more can I do? I surrender myself."

You have to come home to your real Self. You have to live from your heart. Then your eyes will be refreshed so that you come to look at life through the eyes of God. Truth is not partial to anyone—it is universal. Initially, there may be a reaction that feels horrible, but it is all part of coming clean of delusion.

Just continue to immerse your energy and your mind into the discovery of the Truth. The greatest opportunity for anyone facing difficulties in life is to use such intense experiences to inquire into who the sufferer is. Who is bearing the brunt of the impact of whatever the experience may be? This is not a cynical approach or an avoidance of life. No, by really taking your attention back and zeroing in on the center of gravity where the throb of this hurt is the most intense, you assert your true power again, which is always with you.

If you stick to the inquiry, you will make a true nonphenomenal discovery: you will recognize that you cannot find yourself as a suffering entity. Instead, it is revealed to you that you are this space-like awareness within which this noise is playing out. But the awareness that you are is itself neither participating nor touched by any of it. What freedom to discover this Truth.

Since your life is dedicated to the discovery of your true, inherent freedom, you also don't need to apologize for not being in sync with people whose lives have not turned toward Truth. Walk your own way. A greater power is with you. Is that power also with whomever it is you are having difficulties with? It is, even though people may not be conscious of this. Just be firm in the heart's Truth, and its power will touch all those around you.

On Being Single

It is a strong concept for many people that it is better to be in a relationship than to be single. I have even been asked if there is a role in society for people who are single. To this I have to say, of course there is! But you are not a "single person." Rather, as the Self, you are a singular Being. Be *That*.

Nothing is wrong with any expression of life. Whether you're celibate, dating, married, or divorced—it doesn't matter. I saw one woman sitting between two men who seemed to be great friends. With a grin, she said, "Mooji, this is my ex-husband, and this is my next husband." Life is playing its fiddle.

A single person—what's the problem? The "person" is the problem, not the "single." Sometimes we don't know how lucky we are to be able to use our aloneness and the space it gives us to grow in wisdom. Use the time on your own to develop inwardly, so that you overcome the ego that shows up, among other things, as the tendency to need a connection with another person to reach a state of fulfillment. When the ego is in charge, we are more likely to come from a place of desperation when we enter into a relationship.

If you use your time well while you're single to get grounded in the true Self, then the perfume that arises from you may naturally attract other beings. But if your search for Truth remains merely a strategy for attracting someone to you, then the ego is still being allowed to camouflage itself.

Should a relationship be written in your destiny, it will happen naturally and won't be governed by a desperate need to be with someone so that you feel okay about yourself. You will have outgrown such delusions. Only then is a relationship really beautiful.

ULTIMATELY WE ARE ALL ALONE, BUT UPON THE REALIZATION OF THE SELF, WE DISCOVER THAT WE ARE ALONE AS THE UNIVERSE.

Many married people want to be single for a while. I think that every long-term relationship would benefit from a period during which the couple separates for a little bit—not as a rule, but voluntarily. It doesn't even have to be thought of as a separation. This doesn't mean you head straight to Las Vegas or take up with other people. It's a time to find your peace in aloneness and to check in again with what is important for you.

Everybody starts out single. No one is born married! We first learn to move through life in this way. Being single can be a beautiful time, or it can be a terrible time—all that depends on your mind-set. Each moment, you have the power to determine your experience. You, the beingness, have the power to keep your energy in the silence of your Being or to go with conditioned thought. In childhood, we are acculturated to wanting to grow up into Ken and Barbie. But if we don't shed this conditioning, we will miss out on the beauty of being alone.

Ultimately we are all alone, but upon the realization of the Self, we discover that we are alone as the Universe.

Wrap Yourself Around the Eternal

You may ask how to forgive those who hurt us, especially those we love and thought could never hurt us. There are two ways to feel hurt. One is a response to people doing hurtful things. The other is getting hurt even without anyone having had the intention of hurting us. We get hurt by projecting on others and then blaming our feelings on them when our projections don't get met.

Maybe we're just expecting too much from the ones we love. If we tend to load a lot of expectations on people's shoulders and assume they will fulfill those needs absolutely, then we are bound to get disappointed. We are simply expecting too much from what a 'person' is. It is not that we stop trusting—of course, trust is important—but we need to get out of the habit of pouring ourselves into anyone. Our bubbles have to burst in order for us to go anywhere beyond them. And so, life is doing you the favor of letting you down in certain ways to encourage you to find what cannot let you down. But seek even *that* without expectations.

How can you forgive people? By discovering the Self. Once you discover the Self, you can overlook all these things—no big deal. You no longer expect anything from anyone. When you don't *expect*, see how much easier it is to forgive the people you love.

What can you possibly want so much from another person? There are some people you think will never hurt you—and then they do. Don't take life so personally. Let us be a bit lighter in the way we move through life. Find that place in which you are no longer dependent on another, a place where you may marinate in your own true Self.

Remember that no human being is without shortcomings. Even if you were in the company of an angel, eventually they might tick you off about something, and you would say, "Look, I'm sorry but you have to go. Get thee back to heaven!"

But maybe instead of kicking the angel out the door, just acknowledge that no one is perfect and you won't take it personally if it turns out that the person is merely human after all. Drop your expectations of people and stop trying to entwine them.

Wrap yourself around the eternal. In the greater space of immutable awareness, people's seeming shortcomings will not impact you so deeply. In fact, you come to see that these things don't truly exist.

Come home to Truth, and your relationships will not suffer. Rather, every aspect of your relationships will benefit, whether it is in your life partnerships or your encounters with people in everyday life, at work, or with friends and family. All will be infused with wisdom, light, and a sense of spaciousness.

So many people respond by opening up when they feel themselves to be in the presence of a human being who is empty—not empty in a psychological sense, but in a pure sense. We feel real emptiness in that pure state of no-mind. It's a beautiful state of neutrality that also exercises a powerful attraction on others. So few people are empty—everybody is full! Our lives have become claustrophobic, full of clutter, hemmed in by appointments to keep, by all that we have to remember to do, by so many pressures.

So this is my advice: Don't separate relationships from Truth. Otherwise relationships will just be a kind of trudge to the graveyard in familiar company. Don't just "have a relationship"—man and woman, you and me, Tarzan and Jane. A living relationship isn't like this. Rather, a relationship in Truth is a model for consciousness that actually helps us come home and discover Truth.

Whether it's with family, in romance, or in how we relate to peers, all such intense or prolonged interactions tend to expose what's unreal. So work with whatever these relationships bring up. Find out what's broken. Take responsibility in the truest sense of the word. Work to be free of all notions that are keeping you back from stepping into oneness. The empty one is a good candidate for happiness in a relationship, because such a one won't even think of love as a relationship. They are just relating spontaneously from the unicity of Being. This is the greatness of consciousness, the magnificence of Being.

Often what is needed within families
is a shift of perspective.
Stop putting the focus on waiting for *them* to change.
You must be the change that you wish to see in the world.
When you change, there is something
in each of us that knows this.
It's not pretense. It's not a new strategy.
It's not a new disguise.
Your whole energy system is behaving differently.
You will not be stirred up so easily.
You will not let yourself
be taken advantage of or anything like that.
A new light, a new understanding and wisdom,
is functioning now.
Each day it becomes brighter and clearer.
It may not happen overnight, but things will be different.
Now Mom is God!
Something inside knows:
Wait a minute, God has moved into the house
and he's living in Mom now.

Truth and Family

WHEN YOU ARE discovering the Truth of who you are, you also discover a kind of impersonal intimacy. I know this may seem like a strange way of putting it, because normally we think of intimacy as something very personal indeed. What I mean by *impersonal intimacy* is that this love does not require a history, because it recognizes itself in each one immediately. The ego sense is different: it needs time to see if you are a good person, if you are fulfilling expectations, and so on. This happens in all areas of life, but it can be especially strong in the family realm.

Personal intimacy comes with all these conditions, but the love that springs from the heart does not require any of that. If you see people only as personalities or as the role you expect them to fulfill, you may or may not like them or get along with them. That's not to say that everyone is the same: we are One in essence, but each one is unique in expression. When the Self is found, the sense of individuality may still be there, but it no longer smells of ego.

Your consciousness becomes much more subtle. It recognizes that all impressions are momentary and that everything is in motion, but consciousness itself is stable, complete, and content. The Self recognizes itself inside of each form. When we can love like this, without demands or expectations, we move in a sphere of natural harmony.

Make Some Time to Discover the Timeless

As people discover their true nature, many of them wonder how to be with their families, especially their children. Many questions arise: "Is it possible to discover the Self even though my children are so demanding of my time and energy? Will I still be able to look after my family as I am disappearing as a person? How can I share this discovery with my loved ones?"

Tremendous changes have arisen in families because of satsang. Although it is not the goal of inquiry, entire family dynamics have shifted as one person in the family begins to discover their true nature. This change starts with you—you must come into the realization of the Self, because you are the one who is open to it. Take your full receiving of it, and then let the light share itself how it wants. Don't worry so much about your loved ones getting it right now; don't even expect that they understand you. Just fully imbibe, fully merge in this understanding as much as you're able. It's not a case of you get it and then they get it, but you may be surprised at how the family dynamics change as you open up.

If you are looking with very motherly or fatherly physical eyes, you may be wondering where to find space for introspection in all this family responsibility. You have to find the space in your heart. There is no situation that, by itself, blocks you from the realization of the Self; we just believe that it does. We make up our own defense to stay in prison. Of course, we don't do that deliberately, but in some way, we are overcaring, so the wisdom inside us is not coming out enough for us to know how to captain our ship and guide the situation.

Sometimes one has to step away from overcaring, from overworrying. How wise is your guidance likely to be if it is rooted in projections, expectations, fear, and these things so rife in the realm of the ego-mind. Sometimes we are minding too much, taking more responsibility on our shoulders than necessary. You will continue to love your family and to care for them, but you will also come to see that they have their own path in this life. Wisdom helps you make that important discernment.

Respect your space. Children can be demanding, particularly for single parents, but don't make excuses for your limited time. Even if it's only five minutes, be fully in those five minutes. The Supreme knows—it will do in your five minutes what may take someone else five hours, because that is the time you have. What I am telling you is that it *is* possible.

Often what is needed within families is a shift of perspective. Stop putting the focus on waiting for *them* to change. You must be the change that you wish to see in the world. When you change, there is something in each of us that knows this. It's not pretense. It's not a new strategy. It's not a new disguise. Your whole energy system is behaving differently. You will not be stirred up so easily. You will not let yourself be taken advantage of or anything like that. A new light, a new understanding and wisdom, is functioning now. Each day it becomes brighter and clearer. It may not happen overnight, but things will be different. Now Mom is God! Something inside knows: *Wait a minute, God has moved into the house and he's living in Mom now.* The rules have changed.

Something is taking care of you. Don't be distracted. When this spiritual food is given to you, don't immediately give it to someone else. You eat. You need this nourishment. They can eat after you. Don't feed them while you are starving in the corner.

You must take up the gauntlet. You are in a very good position already because your heart is called by Truth. Tremendous strength can come and change the way circumstances are unfolding. Maybe the situation even begs for it. This reminds me of one story about a girl who came to see Papaji.

My Head at Your Feet

This young woman was in a relationship with a man who used to beat her. One day she simply ran away and went to India. There she met Papaji and lived with him for some time. Eventually she had to go home for an important family occasion. She had never told her family the full situation, and her boyfriend was still in contact with them, so he also knew she would be coming home soon.

She approached Papaji and said, "I need to go home, but I am afraid of what will happen with my boyfriend. He might really try to beat me up, especially because I just left without a word."

Papaji said, "No, no, you go. Everything is fine." She trusted his words and boarded the plane. But as the plane was landing, she began to feel very anxious. As she collected her luggage and came through customs, it became even worse. Then she spotted him some seventy yards away, and he started to come toward her—at first walking and then running.

She thought he was going to attack her, and everything inside her froze. She didn't see her family anywhere, only this man running toward her. Then suddenly he fell and put his head on her feet and held them. She was completely shocked! This was totally out of character for this man.

She was still afraid, but when he stood up, she said, "What were you doing? Why did you do that?"

He said, "I was so happy to see you and ran to hug you. But when I came toward you, it was like some power pushed me down to the ground and put my head at your feet!"

I have never forgotten this story because I know this power, and it is always here. When somehow in your heart you have chosen that this life is for freedom, this life is for Truth, then great power comes to support you. Great power comes to support this understanding being established in you. Your life becomes bright, fresh, and strong in a true way.

This is my blessing for you.

Your Life Has to Feel Right for You

Many beings searching for Truth face pressure from their families, particularly their parents, to be a certain way. I understand the family pressure also. They want the best for you according to their own way of perceiving things. But often they overlook the important factor that your life has to feel right for you. This pressure to be a certain way may lead to a whole realm that can seem quite suffocating—guilt, lies, heaviness, confusion, even estrangement from your family.

WHEN YOU HAVE CHOSEN THAT THIS LIFE IS FOR FREEDOM, THEN GREAT POWER COMES TO SUPPORT YOU.

Many people have gone through the experience of letting down some expectations; I had this with my mother. But once you go through this, if they are genuine, the genuine side of them must come back to life. But some people are also very stubborn, perhaps even arrogant or ignorant in these matters, at least for a while. But this is also a play of consciousness, and if it plays like that, just stay true to what you know is right in your heart.

The Fifth Step

I had just come into this realization of Truth. For a while, my mother felt that my rebirth was to her liking, but once she saw that my spiritual and religious expression was not aligned with her particular form of Christianity, she was not as happy. With a 2,000-year-old story to reinforce her views, her attacks at that time could be quite strong and painful.

One day she called me down from my room and said, "Please read this passage from the Bible." Now, I was used to this. In the community I grew up in, it wasn't unusual for parents to say "read this passage from the Bible for me." I actually felt touched that she had chosen to share with me in this way again. I started reading, "Then the Lord rained down burning sulfur on Sodom and Gomorrah . . ."

When I finished reading the passage, she simply said, "Thank you." I gave the Bible back to her and started to go upstairs to my room. But when I got to the fifth step, something suddenly hit—*bam!*—and I understood that she had just made a huge judgment. Her showing me this particular passage from the Scriptures had revealed what her mind had been thinking about me. She had wanted to put a bitter taste in my mouth, *Remember what happened to Sodom and Gomorrah.*

Upon reaching the fifth step, my whole being shook, and I was frozen in place for a few seconds. Then, I found myself running back down the steps and saying, "Mom, why did you ask me to read this particular passage?"

She started to answer innocently, "Well, I don't know." And I felt such anger both for her attack and for her denial. It was an acid feeling inside. That incident was actually a turning point in my relationship with my mother, though it would take a few more years before the new direction in our relationship would become apparent.

I carried this resentment for some time. I even declined to contribute when my brothers and sisters collected money for her flight from Jamaica back to London.

Once she arrived in London, my mother would sometimes watch Christian religious programing on TV, but if the church was of a different denomination than her own, she would mutter things like, "Oh yes, they are really on the way to hell, they are!"

One time when I was sitting next to her and heard her pass judgment in this way, I felt the old anger rising up again, but instead of reciprocating by passing judgment on her, I found myself saying, "Mom, if Jesus were sitting next to you right now, would he be pleased with you for what you have just said?"

A lot of anger was coursing through me, but some power inside transmuted the anger and found a way to approach her calmly with the language of the Bible.

"What, what?" she replied.

And so I repeated, "You just said that those people on TV are all destined for hell. Would Jesus be pleased with you for passing judgment in this way?"

"I said this?"

"Yes, you did.

"Oh, that's not good!"

I was surprised by her response. My heart immediately softened toward her. From that day forward, the nature of our interactions changed. Previously, I hadn't seen that her bark was fiercer than her bite. She was not as narrow-minded as I had always thought. There was great humility present, being masked by a fiercely judgmental facade. Underneath, there was actually something quite gentle.

This was how the whole relationship between me and my mother improved. She recently passed away, but for many years, among all of her children, I was the one who was the most relaxed with her. If she made any foolish, narrow-minded remarks, I had no fear of them, nor was I hesitant to call her on it. I would say, "You are such a hypocrite!" and she would laugh.

However, in spite of the change in my relationship with my mother, to this day, if I have to go up some stairs, sometimes a strong feeling is triggered on the fifth step. I almost stop, as if something catches hold of me. The feeling is quickly followed by a sense of *Ah, okay. Phew . . . gone.* It passes through me quickly, because I know that the physical contraction that has been triggered actually has nothing to do with my mother, and that the person she had been back then ceased to exist long before she passed away. In fact, that person had perhaps only ever existed in my perception of her.

Still there's that fifth step—what to do about it? Nothing but to forget about it! The fifth step is nothing at all!

Don't wait for anything before discovering who you truly are—certainly not for circumstances, the past, or your family's attitudes to change. If some memory is bothering you, drop it! If you can't, then take it into your inquiry. Sometimes you are living in a memory of something that someone may have done. It may not even have been intentional, but it struck deeply, and it became something you carry for the rest of your life. Then, you finally approach that person and say, "All my life I've been suffering because of what you did."

SO MUCH OF OUR MEMORY IS BASED UPON OUR PERCEPTION OF EVENTS THAT CHANGING OUR PERCEPTION ESSENTIALLY CHANGES THE PAST.

"Why? What did I do to you?"

"You know! That day you took my candy, and you gave it to my sister! I knew from then on that you loved her more than you loved me!"

"But I gave you another piece of candy that I thought you liked better!"

"Yes, but I wanted *the other one.*"

Many memories are made of exactly such misinterpretations. Lives are built around things like this. Suffering is created around things like this. And such memories can become magnified and snowball to monstrous proportions. But if you could look at them in their original form, you would laugh at them. So much of our memory is based upon our perception of events that changing our perception essentially changes the past.

Whatever may have happened in the past, you have to recognize it and leave it aside. Dwelling on memories is not in service to you. Nothing benefits from it. Does something like the fifth step stop you from being the Self? Absolutely not! But if you think, *I'm never going to be perfect until I conquer the fifth step*, then the fifth step becomes a big problem for you. Yet, it is nothing at all!

Traumatic memories are like seeds in the mind, but these seeds require watering with attention and belief in order to grow—and you have been pouring it on. Don't pour on the water. Even thinking that it is important enough to eliminate gives it what it needs to grow. Just forget about it.

Remember your Self.
You are *now*. That *was*.
The Self is not "was." It *is*.
It is not memory. Memory functions in it.
All these things, all the stories are in it,
but it is untouched.
You are this untouched one.

When Life Gives You a Shove

A woman came to satsang and told a story about her friend whose husband had passed. The husband's will had stipulated that the house would technically belong to the children, but she could continue to reside there for the rest of her life. But then her son threw her out of the house!

To have your own son throw you out—can you imagine such a thing? Your children were in your house, you attended to their every need, and now you are out on the street. But don't think that it's necessarily a bad thing. It may appear to be a sad thing, but for many, such events were the trigger to start acknowledging their own nature as free beings. If her heart is in the right place, she will make good use of this experience so that one day she will look back in gratitude and say, "Thank you, life, for the actions of my son. Thank you not only for my being thrown out of my house, but also for my being thrown out of my life!"

The divine Truth throws you out of yourself and enters your absence. You want to be something. You want to get somewhere. You want to cling to something—but sometimes life just throws you out. It may not make sense if you are primarily a rational-minded person. When you imagine what it would be like to be thrown out of your house and out of your life, it may seem like a terrible thing, but to actually experience it can be pure joy.

Rather than just being, we spend a lot of time thinking our lives by imagining, projecting, and reliving memories as a substitute for the here and now. In this process, we are elsewhere with our minds, and we miss out on the magnificence of life and the reality of the one true Self. So we all need a bit of a push sometimes.

This push may even come in the form of something seemingly mundane, such as a bird pooping on your head—*splat!* That might just be the very thing that gives you the courage you need to turn your life around. It is grace falling from that branch above.

A man in satsang once told the following story.

Nothing There for Me

In the area where I lived with my partner, we had a large group of friends who were like family to me. People would come to us with their troubles, seeking our advice. We had always been supportive and loyal to them.

Then one day, out of the blue, I found my partner in bed with someone else. I broke up with her immediately. I was so distraught. But then *ding!* I thought, *At least I have my friends to turn to!*

I looked in my address book. *Okay, I'll ring George.* "Hey, George, how you doing? Can I talk to you?"

"Sorry, not right now, man. Can I call you back? I'm a bit busy at the moment."

No problem, I thought, *I'll call Matt.* "Hey, Matt, how you doing?"

"This is Matt's voicemail. I'll be gone for a week. I'll get back to you then."

Okay, then, I'll call Susan. "Susan, hi. This is David."

"Hi David, what's up?"

"Can I talk to you about something?"

"Wow, David, I'm not in a good head-space at all. I'd be the last person you'd want to talk to at this moment. Nothing personal, you understand. Maybe some other time?"

And so it went as I moved through the list. These were all the friends I thought I could count on because I had always been ready to leave everything aside for them. But on that day of torment and unprecedented anguish, when it was finally my turn to call on them, no one was available. What could I do?

I was in such a painful place that I had to go away. Then, alone in a strange hotel room far from home, I saw that I was like a leaf floating on a river, and that I was sinking down fast. In my mind, I was screaming, *No, no! I don't want to go down alone into the muck at the bottom of my life. No, please! George, where are you? Matt, where are you? Susan, where are you? Mildred? Frank? Ahhhh!*

No one was there to save me. Then, suddenly it all looked so different than it had the moment before. *Whoa! Wow!* I had arrived at the place that I had always been afraid to reach—the very bottom of my life—it was sublime!

I was so happy that I wanted to send an email to all my friends, thanking them for *not* being there for me—not as a cynical dig, but with sincere gratitude, because what I really needed was to be alone. I needed that moment just for me.

My mind wanted to hold the hand of a friend, but no one was there for me. Now my heart is not resentful. Instead, I feel so much appreciation for them and gratitude to life for their not having been there for me. For once, nothing was there for me—only nothing-ness.

This man had hit rock bottom and was totally alone. Yet for the first time ever he felt really alive, and his heart was overflowing with love.

When people say their lives are falling apart, I know what it usually means: something auspicious has just happened. This falling apart usually leads people to a better place—unless they have the kind of mind that holds onto a negative interpretation of events. If so, they will suffer their experience. But eventually, they may still grow from it and recognize something that has been there all along. Such a coming-apart-at-the-seams can be the catharsis that throws you back inside of yourself, serving as a mirror that reveals the truth of who you are. This dissolution is a great moment. So don't lose this chance by misinterpreting it to be something that should not have happened.

WHEN PEOPLE SAY THEIR LIVES ARE FALLING APART, I KNOW WHAT IT USUALLY MEANS: SOMETHING AUSPICIOUS HAS JUST HAPPENED.

There is a saying: *The barn burned down, and now the sky can be seen.* Sometimes your barn has to burn down and your treasures have to be taken from you in order for you to come back to life again. The mind wants you to make things secure, to surround yourself with familiar things. You can see those reassuring reference points all around you, but a moment may come when they can no longer be found. This can be the greatest blessing.

Our Western culture makes living in a state of contentment so difficult. We have all been conditioned to feel that we must have an underlying problem that has to be overcome before we can be free. Often we blame our circumstances:

"I'm a mess because life has treated me unkindly!"

"My family did this to me!"

"It is all the fault of the government! It's the police!"

 Or, we may also blame ourselves:

"No, it's me doing it to me! It's my mind!"

"I'm not devotional enough."

"I don't have enough focus. I don't practice as much as I should."

Our culturally imparted belief in our own victimhood and in the need to become different from what we presently are makes us defensive and pessimistic. If you look with the eyes of Truth, however, you will discover that often there really is no problem. Rather than stemming from anything significant, the sense of disquiet is just the result of a dissatisfied mind-set. In a sense, we are dependent on problems: we need to be sick, we need to be burdened. Some people are only happy when they are complaining, only content being miserable.

These may seem to be hard, strange, and even painful things to hear, but there is a truth in them that wants to emerge.

The one who is free has shed the worn-out costume of person-hood—but not in disgust, not reactively. It's just that through the imperative of a deeper seeing and understanding, people come to see: *I am not the one acting, reacting, or interacting.* Rather, something seems to be doing it, and you are the one observing these movements.

In the beginning, you will still be feeling yourself to be in the driver's seat. Then, as you grow in wisdom, you will more frequently see yourself as the passenger, the audience to what is taking place. Finally, you may come to see that you are actually the witness of both the sense of driver and of passenger. There is no name for that state of pure awareness, but we call it freedom, awakening, enlightenment, Buddha nature, Christ light. Call it what you will, the names are not important. They are only indicators.

I like to say that in satsang, we may start out with hundreds of people, but at the end, there is only presence. From person to presence—there is a space of inner understanding that is *you*, and it is neither a library nor a hard drive. You don't need to *be* somebody, but keep that as your secret. Outside, you may still appear to "be somebody," but inside you are completely cooked, utterly empty.

Get accustomed to feeling empty. Observe how life is not made but rather unfolds out of this spaciousness. How? Think about all the hair on your head: Did it grow out of a thick clump of hair under the scalp? No, there's nothing there. Where did it come from?

Everything is like that!

Where are the flowers that will soon appear on a tree? They will simply blossom from the tree itself. It won't have to go anywhere else to get them. Your life is simply flowering, unfolding by itself. There is no "tree" inside a tree, no "cloud" inside a cloud, no "horse" inside a horse. And there is no "person" inside a human body. There is just consciousness and the dance of the life force. Come to recognize the simplicity of all of this and bask in immutable joy.

With this fresh discovery and understanding
of your real Self as pure awareness,
you are able to feel your apartness from
the dynamic activity of the psychological mind.
You are aware of all those old habits of mind,
how constricted they make you feel,
and how they seem to eclipse the sense of presence.
With the power of self-inquiry,
you are able to break free from this spell of delusion
and win your Self back.

Healing Through Transcendence

SOME BEINGS COME to satsang having suffered greatly in life, perhaps from illness or from physical, sexual, or emotional trauma. They have found some solace and strategies for coping with their suffering, and this is good. But they reach a point where they don't want to just cope. One person asked me, "I want to remove myself from the tentacles of my story, but the scenes seem to play themselves out in an endless loop. Can I make it stop?"

I say, yes, it can stop *now*. But you must see *exactly* what it is that can stop, for your vision must be clear and your intentions genuine if this delusion is to be dispelled. Belief in a false identity can end today. Suffering and emotional wounds cannot truly be healed and transcended by means of intellectual reasoning. Transcendence must be attained through understanding.

Unless we contemplate ourselves deeply, we continue giving credence both to the way we experience life personally and to the personalities we believe ourselves to be. Through the force and grip of your identification with memories and traumas, the mind in its psychological aspect has been holding your attention and sucking energy from you long enough.

If you are suffering from something that happened in the past, this suffering is caused by your identification with those memories, projections, and images. Many people have lived through traumatic experiences in childhood or adolescence and have been able to use those very experiences to overcome the obstacles that were created. But others are still carrying the weight of victimhood around their necks. Some even continue to nurse a grudge when the perpetrator has long ago mended their ways. They may even be getting along with that person now, but there is a part of them that is still suffering from those painful, personal memories.

IF YOU DON'T PRESS "SAVE," YOU WON'T HAVE TO PRESS "DELETE." JUST STAY NEUTRAL AND LET THE MEMORIES PLAY WHILE YOU REMAIN ROOTED IN TIMELESSNESS.

We all must realize that pure awareness—the Self—remains untouched by even the most difficult memories or traumas that may surface. Yet, simultaneously, we live the dynamic expression of awareness, which manifests as life, as what we call existence—a world where we experience time, memory, and the sense of self and where we are also able to look at issues such as healing emotional wounds.

Soon you will see that the mind's tendency to act as a zoom lens is also being intensified by your belief in that perspective and by sheer force of habit. Once you are able to see through the mind's fickleness and tendency to focus in on and obsess about problems, it is easier to let go and return to panoramic seeing. Even while engaged in everyday life, you remain in the position of the neutral and imageless witness. And, because you will be experiencing life through and as presence itself, you will not dig into the past or project into the future anymore. All the movements called life then appear as if they are writing on water—even moments later they cannot be read.

If you don't press "save," you won't have to press "delete." Just stay neutral and let the memories play and occupy the space they need to fill while you remain rooted in timelessness.

SELF-INQUIRY GUIDANCE

Stay as Awareness

While some concepts may be easily turned away from and just dissolve without any fuss, if an issue or problem is demanding your constant attention and there is no easy turning away from it, then you will have to face that entrenched negative pattern, that *vasana*.

Expose it and lay it bare in the light of self-inquiry.

You are not what you perceive, so immediately you know you cannot be your experiences. You are not even the one to whom those experiences—good or bad—happen.

So who are you then? Stop and look inward.

Verify what I am pointing you toward.

Direct your attention away from the phenomenal mind into that empty space that remains when everything definable and knowable is discarded as unreal.

Now be confirmed in that inwardness—this is your indivisible Self.

You are the awareness within which everything appears and disappears, but the awareness itself isn't aroused by any phenomenon, nor has it ever arisen.

From this awareness Self, you are even aware of the comings and goings of consciousness. Therefore, you must be earlier than

the consciousness that embodies the capacity for the functioning of perception, earlier than the space in which phenomena
are perceived as they take the shape of something-ness and dissolve again into nothing-ness.

Stay as awareness.

Why would we look in this way? Because inquiring into these
questions—*From where is all this being seen? With what identity
am I looking? Who am I, the perceiver?*—is the most important
step we can take toward that inner recognition of our formless
nature. And if you don't clarify and confirm your true position as
the formless ultimate seer, you will continue to identify with the
phenomenal experiencer, the ego. Then some thought, memory,
or event will inevitably come along and grab your attention. You
will again feel thrown off balance and find yourself sliding into
the familiar yet unstable state of personhood. In so falling, you
will have missed the opportunity to notice that even *memory* is
phenomenal.

The End of Suffering

You may object that you don't believe in the end of suffering. Somehow you don't believe it is possible. I say, don't ever
believe anything, because belief pertains to something that is
in the future. You have a strong belief in the past as well. But
it is finished—it is only being perpetuated by your belief and
interest in your memories.

It is as if on meeting for the first time, all you want to show
me is the photo album of your childhood. I say, "But we are
here now."

You say, "This was me when I was six, seven, and, look, fifteen."

I say, "But you are here now! You are better and greater than any photo album. You are fresh. The album is not fresh."

You are fresh, but something doesn't trust that. You want to retain something, as if that were to make the ground you stand upon more solid.

Why are we afraid to just be what we really are? Because if you say to yourself, "I have to let go of my story," it feels like you are losing something valuable, and this is seen as increasing your suffering. But actually, this is how you let go of your suffering.

I would often hear Papaji recount the following story of one man who was speaking to the sage Sri Nisargadatta Maharaj, saying, "Sir, I have been listening to you, and I believe every word you say. But to be honest, in my case, I am always experiencing suffering."

SOMETHING KEEPS INSISTING, "HELP! I'M IN TROUBLE!" I SAY: NOT ONLY ARE YOU *IN* TROUBLE, YOU *ARE* TROUBLE!

Maharaj replied, "No, what you are saying is not true. You are not experiencing suffering. You are suffering your *experiencing*."

Suffering is not a thing. Pain is, but suffering is not. It smacks of an attitude that shows up when we feel trapped in the personal and are lamenting, "Life is against me!" and, "I don't know what I am going to do!" Then we create a sense of suffering with which to torment ourselves.

The sense of identity is at the root of all suffering. The trouble is in our concept of 'I.' As soon as we acknowledge this, genuine change can happen, but something keeps insisting, "Help! I'm in trouble!" I say: Not only are you *in* trouble, you *are* trouble! Then you may think, "Oh, he's insulting me!" when in fact I am helping you.

It is strenuous to work on the personal level, because personhood is a high-maintenance state—and it's not even a true state.

The Old Lady in the Closet

Once it happened that two friends found each other after having lost contact for many years. They immediately arranged to spend several days together at a beautiful house that one of them owned in the country. They were both excited, because they had been close at one time and had a lot of catching up to do.

When the friend who was visiting arrived at the house, her friend welcomed her enthusiastically: "Welcome darling! It is so wonderful to see you again!" They sat down and shared news and stories for a good few hours. It was a beautiful reunion.

It was getting late, and the visiting friend was now feeling tired, so her host said, "I'll take you to your room." She took the bags upstairs to the guest room. They said goodnight and went to bed in their separate rooms.

The guest was getting ready for bed and went to the closet to put her things away. As she opened the door, she jumped back and shrieked—there was an old lady in the closet! The old lady was just sitting there very calmly, wearing white gloves and holding a purse on her lap. Thinking that it must be a ghost, the guest ran downstairs screaming in terror.

Her friend, hearing the commotion, ran out of her room, asking, "What's going on?"

The trembling guest replied, "Love, I'm sorry. The room is very nice, but there's an old lady, a ghost, sitting in the closet!"

The friend replied, "What in the world are you talking about? I built this house and have lived here for many years. No one ever died in this house. How could there possibly be the ghost of an old lady in the closet?"

But the guest swore to what she had seen. So, her friend said, "Let's go have a look." Slowly, the guest composed herself and found the courage to follow her friend back to the room.

The friend opened the closet and smiled. She could immediately see what had happened. There was a purse and some gloves lying on a chair inside the closet with a dress hanging right above it. With the light of the moon shining in and the shadows of the trees swaying in the wind, it indeed could have appeared to be the figure of an old lady, especially if one was very tired and had an easily excitable mind.

The friend asked her guest, "Where's the old lady?" The guest looked in and saw the bag, the gloves, the chair, and the dress. She instantly realized her mistake and understood how she could have misinterpreted what she had seen as being a ghost.

"Oh, my! I have really managed to freak myself out and rattle your nerves. I'm so sorry. What a runaway mind I have! I should be able to sleep now. Good night." Both women went off to bed.

In the morning, when the guest came down for breakfast, she asked her friend, "How did you sleep?"

"I slept very well, how about you?"

"I didn't sleep a single wink."

"Why not? What happened?"

"The old lady is still in the closet!"

"What in heaven's name are you talking about?" said the host. "I thought that we settled this matter last night!"

"She's there, I tell you! I don't know how it can be possible, but she is."

So, once again, they went up together to look in broad daylight. "Look—it's just a dress. Should I move it?"

"Yes, please move it, and take the gloves and purse out of the closet altogether and put them in your room."

The day passed well enough, and the guest was even able to take a nap in the room at midday. When night fell, they again went to their rooms.

The next morning the guest said, "I'm leaving today."

"Why, what happened?"

"I'm sorry, but—the old lady—she's still disturbing me. I know that you moved all the things, but every time I close my eyes at night, I see her again, just sitting there staring back at me."

This story makes us laugh, doesn't it? How foolish the visitor seems, seeing something when nothing is there. We may not like to admit it, but we are a bit like this. People say, "This thing keeps coming up, and it is really troubling me." You are then guided to look at it in the mirror of self-inquiry, and you discover and confirm that there is nothing there. There is no 'person' inside to be an actual victim. Without an actual victim, the troubling thing dissipates like a cloud on a summer's day. You are so relieved and grateful! But soon after you report, "You know, I could see everything so clearly, but then I was just sitting here and my mind came back strongly." Or you say, "My mind is fine in meditation, but I know it's just waiting to catch me as soon as I go to work."

When this happens, I can only ask, as I've asked so many times before, "What is this mind that you speak about? Who is this 'person' who is suffering?" And I can remind you, yet again, that it is all illusion—as unreal as the imaginary lady in the closet. When these strong thoughts or feelings arise, we know the terror, but what we really need to do is to look at the one who is terrified. Each time we look for the one who is suffering the experience, it is discovered that nobody at all is there to be suffering. It is all a figment of our imagination.

This is the real fruit of self-inquiry. Not only does it expose the myth of egoic identity, but it also reveals the binding power of unquestioned belief and the mind's fear of discovering its own unreality. Self-inquiry actually shows how ego gets shaped and fueled by steady and persistent attention and belief. In this way, we come to see that the ego itself is merely another phenomenon.

When you realize that the personal entity itself is phenomenal, it is an amazing discovery. Often when someone discovers, "My God, there's nothing there!" they are stunned into silence or burst into laughter or tears—but the laughter is without a joke and the tears are not of sadness.

This beautiful discovery is being made all over the world. In most cases, however, when I see those people the following day, they are all wrapped up in thinking again. And when I ask, "How is it all going?" Guess what? They reply, "I don't know. It's the old lady again." What is the difference between the story of the old lady and the version of it playing out in your own life?

With this fresh discovery and understanding of your real Self as pure awareness, you are able to feel your apartness from the dynamic activity of the psychological mind. You are aware of all those old habits of mind, how constricted they make you feel, and how they seem to eclipse the sense of presence. With the power of self-inquiry, you are able to break free from this spell of delusion and win your Self back.

Keep Confirming and Verifying

When the ghost of personal identity appears, it is not enough to simply recall your previous insight. Rather than just thinking, *I know that the old lady is unreal* and still somehow going along with the mind's suggestions, you must inquire into this voice each time it arises. In this way, you can choose to remain in the neutral position of the witnessing presence.

As a result, there is going to be a changing over of power from person to presence, which is like a shift from manual to automatic. From this auspicious position of presence, we are aware that we are merely witnessing the phenomena appearing as identity, emotion, projection, fear, or attachment. We observe their fleetingness and, with deeper scrutiny, expose their hollowness.

However, the ability to discern that something is unreal does not necessarily remove its bite. You may find yourself saying, "It is still able to inflict pain upon me." What to do? Each time this happens, you have to confirm and verify again that it is the voice of *the idea you have of who you are*, and not the voice of pure Being. The old lady appears to be there, but only as an illusory entity that has taken up residence within you.

Beware of frustration. Don't say, "Why isn't it going away already? Why do I keep falling back into delusion?" Rather, investigate whether the one who is asking, "Why does it keep on bugging me?" is itself real or not. Who is this one who always feels sorry for itself, who is so given to complaining and asking why it doesn't stop?

Here is where we arrive at the most challenging inquiry, for *this* is the voice that almost all human beings identify with. This is the voice that is more intimate than intimacy, the voice that seems to be helping, when in fact it is the culprit. Over seven billion human beings are walking on the face of the earth today, and almost all of us firmly believe in this false identity.

Applying the story of the old lady in the closet to ourselves might seem a little unfair, because we are not just opening a closet door in adulthood and facing some vague shadows that look like a ghost. Rather, throughout the course of our lives, we have been seeing this old lady and believing she is who we actually are. It's very difficult to dismiss something that we feel to be so unquestionably true. Our belief in this apparition is coursing through our veins. The very air we breathe is thick with this identification. Under such circumstances, who is really prepared to confront this belief when it seems already part of our psychological makeup? And *who* exactly is going to tackle that belief?

I tell this story knowing full well that we are none other than pure consciousness and that we are only vulnerable to this delusion as long as we continue to be in a state of "dream sleep." Only by dreaming up a false identity can we succumb to the spell of these special effects of consciousness. The whole game of existence is meant to give us—often through frustrations, broken dreams, crushed and humbled egos—the opportunity to awaken from illusions and limitations. When we awaken from the waking state—and this is why the term *awakening* is so fitting—it is as though we are awakening from a dream and seeing things as they really are. With the force and clarity of this true seeing, nothing troubles us.

Be in Now *Without* And *Then*

Some seekers report that after periods of great silence and peace, the old noise returns, possibly even worse than it was before, and they feel a great deal of frustration and doubt.

I say, don't run away from all of this. Everyone is running away from what they don't want to feel, away from even the remote possibility of some strong reaction or catharsis.

Hand over your existence to existence. Nothing is going to harm you. Remember that you have chosen Truth; it is the lie that is being burped up, so let it come up! Hold your ground and let this pass. If you don't and you keep on suppressing and delaying, then you have chosen to live with this inner noise. And the lie will remain and will behave in ever more subtle ways, so that, increasingly, you will not even notice it. One could say that listening to the lie is a bit like a boarder who becomes a lover and then begins to dominate you to the extent that they start charging *you* rent.

HAND OVER YOUR EXISTENCE TO EXISTENCE.

Don't resist the waves of nausea anymore. Your own inner satsang will bring all these things up. We can't even imagine how much psychic junk food we have ingested on the journey of life. Now that you have said yes to Truth, you're stepping into the light, which is acting as a kind of purgative, so that all this stuff is coming up spontaneously.

Now you may say, "And then what?"
And then "and then" stops.
Your whole life has been *and then*.
"It was going so well, *and then* . . ."
"I had such a beautiful relationship, *and then* . . ."
"And then this, and then that . . ."
Be in *now* with no more *and then*.
Like this, all suffering will dissipate
in the light of Truth.

When the World Seems Full of Cruelty

From time to time in satsang, people ask why a certain tragedy happened, on either a personal or global scale. They wonder what we can or should be doing to resolve the world's problems. It is in the nature of life that people we care for fall sick or go through times of great difficulty. And it is natural that we feel empathy and are compelled to help in whatever way we can. All this is also part of the play of consciousness. Often we wish for such things not to happen, but do we actually know what people truly need?

In truth, we don't know what is written in the book of life. Sometimes tragic events unfold, and we wrap ourselves in regret and blame, second-guessing ourselves—if only we had done this and not that, then this awful tragedy would not have happened. But we don't know anything at all in these matters. Sometimes illness or tragedy presents a great opportunity for Self-discovery. Consciousness is playing as all of this, and it seems that sometimes things need to go wrong in order for them to go right.

The Self is just oneness, wholeness, even beyond the concept of oneness. In the absorption of the attention into presence and in the purging of old beliefs and other such burdens from the Self, everything becomes reintegrated into wholeness. Out of that wholeness, the unique expression that is the manifest, dynamic expression of the Self comes into harmony with the whole, naturally and spontaneously.

No human being can balance the universe. In fact, the egoic state is one of imbalance. When you are in your natural state, you discover a synchronicity, a sense of oneness with life that you did not create but simply discovered. And it is always better to discover something than to create it. If you create something, you have to maintain and sustain it, and that is going to be a strain and a burden. But what you discover is effortless.

Any idea such as *I wish the world were more balanced* is itself arising within the consciousness that you already are. The body is indeed the instrument through which consciousness tastes experiencing in its myriad forms. It is the vehicle, and it moves within wholeness anyway. Wholeness is naturally balanced, and so powerful is this balance that even the sense of imbalance is within it. Nothing can move outside the cosmic balance.

If you take responsibility for the world's problems, you will never rest. You will always be thinking *Who shall I save next?* because something in you is motivated by guilt and fear, and that is some of the worst baggage to carry. You will feel responsible for the whole world. Relax with that. Let true intuition come spontaneously. It will come when you are not working things out, not casting a projection. You just happen to be walking, and somehow you come in contact with a person, start talking, and then something unfolds by itself that helps.

> WHOLENESS IS NATURALLY BALANCED, AND SO POWERFUL IS THIS BALANCE THAT EVEN THE SENSE OF IMBALANCE IS WITHIN IT.

That is not to say that a sage just stands aside in times of need. If a sage were walking through a town when an earthquake hit, of course he or she would get involved in the rescue efforts. Compassionate acts come naturally to sages (and, indeed, to many human beings under such circumstances), but the difference is that they remain in a natural state of serenity throughout that allows them to be of even greater service. You do not see them wailing at the sight of so much human suffering.

Their serenity and the serenity of the angels are one. And when their work is done, they go their way.

However, a sage also recognizes that it is often through difficult circumstances that Truth is revealed, because such difficulties compel us to look within and beyond our assumed identity. Thus, when the identity of the sufferer is seen through, the whole experience can bring about physical and emotional healing. One of the greatest balms is a peaceful mind, a peaceful being. Such a state of serenity will help you get well and stay well.

My response to people who ask how we can help those who are suffering—whether from poverty, illness, or some other kind of serious deprivation—is to say that the greatest healing is to be the Self. Until we become aware of the Self, we are suffering from a kind of mental illness. We are wandering around lost. How effective can we be in trying to help others under such circumstances?

When we are established in and as our true nature, spontaneously the right response will arise to support the one in need—and it may not lead to what the *mind* thinks is the best outcome.

Some people make it their intention to perform good actions on a broader scale in the world. They sell their homes, travel abroad, and use all that money to try to help people. This is their calling, and it is a worthy one that I support.

But if you don't have that strong pull toward humanitarian work, don't try to create it in yourself by force or from a place of guilt. Better to spend your time finding out who or what you really are. But don't set up programs for yourself, like, *I will find the Self so I can help others.* Let life unfold. Let the movement of the cosmic stream be felt in you and be in its flow. That is good enough.

Sometimes we might feel that this news is a bit disappointing: you really wanted to know whether, by realizing the Self, you would be able to work miracles!

If it is destined that the expression of miracles should arise through a particular body, then it will happen. The one who is awake is so vast, that if such an expression of grace were to arise, they may or may not even be conscious of its having become manifest through them. They don't necessarily know about particular things that happen outside of their own presence, and the miracle doesn't even have to be done intentionally.

Such is the power of the awakened mind.

Let the one who created the world look after it. That one says, "I am neither past nor future, nor even the present. All of this is my dance; all of this plays by itself." Can *you* also speak like that? Can you see the world in this way? Or can you only look down because you are bearing the weight of the world on your shoulders?

When I was a little boy, I saw a picture from Greek mythology of a man carrying the world on his back. He was so bent over with the weight that you could not even see his face. He is called Atlas. Many years later in India, I saw the image of the one they call Nataraj, Lord Shiva, dancing on top of the world. I said, "I like this one!"

So you can either be Atlas and carry the world on your shoulders, or you can dance the dance of existence like Nataraj—and do even that without identification. Don't try to create some kind of shape for your life as if you are shearing it with a pair of clippers. Don't prune down your own life into the shape you think it should be.

Don't be a bonsai, be a mighty oak.

Reorienting Toward Compassion

If your eyes are open and you are not lost in your own private mythology or ideology, you can't help but be aware of the world's pain and suffering. And you don't have to go far to find it: you will see it on display in every village, town, city, and country in the world.

For thousands of years, people have tried to create peace, usually in the name of religion or political doctrines, but they have not yet succeeded. Besides, most of them were not really interested in peace anyway. They were far more focused on attacking competing religions or disputing among themselves, and they often brought politics into religion for their own ends. Of course, this doesn't include everyone who follows those paths, for each path also has genuine seekers of Truth.

So, we may ask, how will a reorientation toward a more compassionate world come about?

Beings have been sitting in satsang for thousands of years, and throughout the ages, great teachers like Buddha and Jesus set beautiful examples of compassion that people follow. Every now and again, these awakened beings come to address this need; they are called to emerge from their inwardness to communicate with their fellow beings. Such benefactors of humankind have not come looking for devotees for themselves. They look for devotees of the Truth—those who are burning to find the Truth in themselves. Yet you may wonder what the fruit of their realization has been, what impact they have had on the world, since we still see so much cruelty and suffering.

The fruit of their satsang is the existence of so many compassionate people in the world who don't just see suffering; their mere witnessing already transforms the scene. There are thousands of beings who, by means of their own sadhana, their own practice, introspection, and meditation, have become very kindhearted. It can be seen in the kindness they extend freely to others. This was very much the case with Papaji.

I remember somebody asking, "Papaji, when will mankind really evolve into the potential that you speak of?" And he said, "When mankind becomes kind man."

Who is kind in this way? If your realization is only mental, personal, and selfish, then it is not complete. It is not true realization. As Sri Ramana Maharshi says, "All good qualities manifest spontaneously in the awakened mind." That is, when you realize the single, undivided Self, there is no need to cultivate these qualities—they are naturally and effortlessly present.

What is the reason for so much cruelty in the world? It is really quite simple: cruelty persists because we consider ourselves to be only the body, our cultural conditioning, and personality. As long as we believe we are just that package, such selfishness will continue to be expressed.

We have often heard that the opposite of love is hate. But perhaps the opposite of love is really selfishness, each one caring only for who they consider themselves to be. This self-centeredness is characteristic of ego, and it is what satsang addresses. The greatest opportunity is for human beings to become aware of themselves as consciousness, as so many have done before us.

Some may say, yes, but Buddha lived 2,600 years ago; Christ, 2,000 years ago; Krishna, around 5,000 years ago; Rama, around 7,000 years ago. How can they still help humanity today?

I challenge you to consider why we can only name examples so distant in time. If I were to ask people how many great athletes they could name, most could count off many. How many great musicians? A long list. Scientists? A shorter one. Dictators? A handful. But how many liberated beings can you name? "Um, Buddha, yes. Uh, Jesus? Jesus—was he?"

PERHAPS THE OPPOSITE OF LOVE IS REALLY SELFISHNESS, EACH ONE CARING ONLY FOR WHO THEY CONSIDER THEMSELVES TO BE.

Actually, it is not true that there have only been a few enlightened beings throughout history. It is simply that we have lacked the maturity to recognize them. There have always been—and there will continue to be—many liberated beings in this world. But not everyone who has realized the Self becomes a teacher. You may not be able to distinguish them—some may even be living on the street. Awakening is not a fashion show.

Some such beings may not look very impressive. They may not fit the image of what a spiritual being should look like. They may seem pretty ordinary, and so we don't tend to notice them as they move about, but they have the power to be where they are needed. In much the same way that trees produce oxygen for the planet even though nobody goes around thanking them, the influence of these inconspicuous ones contributes tremendously to the quality of life.

One of my favorite plants in England is the buddleia bush. They grow very wild, and nobody has to plant them. They'll grow in the rocks, they'll grow on your roof, they'll grow in the cracks in the walls. They'll even grow on railway lines or where there's no water. Strong wind, they'll grow. Nobody goes and buys them. You don't even notice them. But when they flower, the most beautiful butterflies come from all around just to stay with them. All through their flowering season, they remain like that. And they don't need to call out, "Butterflies! I'm ready!"

No, the butterflies come. The two are one.

Those awakened beings are like this. Quietly, quietly, they are blooming.

And as they bloom, all beings seek their company.

Love Is the Perfume of Your Being

It is easy to love everyone when you are the Self. Only then may you begin to see everyone as they truly are, as the Self. But as long as we see each other merely in the personal aspect, conflict will continue to break out. Just look at what this limitation is doing to people and to the earth. Brutality, fear, judgment, and all kinds of projections arise out of this fundamental misunderstanding of our true nature. Yet, the human race also expresses itself with beauty, creativity, love, and aspiration. And all these expressions are the play of consciousness.

It is a question of some urgency in our time that the human race comes into pure Self-knowledge and we start to acknowledge the underlying unity. Such a reorientation toward oneness is the universal medicine. As we begin to recognize this place of purity inside—the Self—we also recognize that the world and all the beings in it are appearing within our own Being. They are not separate from who we are. Seeing with the eye of unity means you also start to see with the eye of love. There is no hierarchy in this love and no strategy about it. This love is always here. It's not even that you are necessarily *doing* anything for it—it becomes impossible *not* to love, because your very nature is love. Then one does not merely love; love is the very perfume of your Being, and you cannot help but exude that fragrance. Our physical bodies are conceived in beingness, in its love. When love flows with wisdom and pure understanding, it engenders real self-respect, and that love makes the world beautiful.

But when we cling to notions of ourselves as mere personalities, a natural friction often sends sparks flying. The sphere of personhood is an aggressive realm in which, despite people's best intentions and aspirations to do good, they often find themselves doing things that are unreasonable or excessive.

Therefore, those who are awake to the Self encourage people to outgrow that limited view of themselves as being mere persons. Our present self-concept is shallow, narrow, and distorted. In truth, we are not bound by any concept; we are the perceiver of all concepts.

Discover your true position as the indivisible Self—this is the advice the sages give to the world. I don't see any other way forward for humankind than heeding this guidance, but the world must be ready to receive and embrace it. The other way is fraught with hardships that will bring difficult times upon us in proportion to our own arrogance. Sometimes difficult times help us return to our natural state. It seems that we have to create intense pain in order to free ourselves from the trap of arrogance. Ultimately, though, the world is good because its origin is divine.

You may ask, "How can you say the world is good when some expressions of consciousness are so brutal?" The ultimate reality is not the way human beings, as body-mind entities, are accustomed to seeing their relationship to the world around them. The ways of the Supreme are inscrutable to the worldly mind. This is a mighty existence, but it is impossible to comprehend its magnificence through this human instrument alone. Life is an amazing game, but one that you will only start to really enjoy once you have become free of life's spell. Only then will you understand that life is not cruel. What capacities we have! So much love, altruism, and brilliance! And, so much hate, selfishness, and confusion. Everything is there as potential. And it's up to us to choose which qualities we will develop in ourselves.

Some rare beings want to go beyond
even the 'I am' presence.
Why would anyone want to go beyond such a
beautiful and harmonious state?
Because, at the deepest level,
even that state of presence is still not you.
The presence is what the fragrance is to a flower.

When you are in a position to witness this sense of presence,
it too is seen as being phenomenal,
and then you are immersed in the unspeakable
—in the Absolute.

You have become the flower, but, paradoxically,
this flower nobody can find.

The Self Alone Is Real

WHEN WE IDENTIFY ourselves with the sense of personhood, we are much like a wave on the surface of the ocean. Rather than resting in the vast space of pure Being, we have become identified with some kind of passing event, thought, or emotion—perhaps a wave of anger, a particular role in our life, or even our entire sense of personhood. The vastness of Being is like an ocean. Each wave is like a lifetime being played out. Wave is ocean, ocean is ocean, but the wave has forgotten its true oceanic Self. In the play of its rising and falling, the wave dreams that it is separate. In reality there can be no separation from the vastness of Being. We merely believe we are separate. Yet it is possible to wake up out of that sense of separation in an instant, for the Truth is distanceless.

Imagine you are just sitting, and perhaps it is a bit hot, so you close your eyes and doze off. Suddenly you're walking down a beach, and the gentle sunshine feels very nice on your skin. Now you're picking up pebbles, and it seems you have already walked a few miles along the beach. You test the waters, and then you jump in. You start to body surf, get dumped by a wave, and feel like you're drowning. But suddenly you wake up from that dream and instantly you are back. "Wait a minute! I've been sitting here all along!" When you awaken, you discover you're not really drowning and you didn't have to walk a few miles back along that beach. All of it happened only in the dream.

Dreams have no existence independent of the dreamer. The dream cannot dream itself, and it has no self-awareness—the dream doesn't know itself to be a dream. It can only be linked to the mind of the dreamer. So, when the dreamer wakes up, the dream is finished.

Waking Up from the Waking State

When you wake up from the waking state into the true life, you come to understand that you have been living in a kind of dream state. The waking state—your daily life—may be perceived as a good dream if it does not trigger a distortion or create some bad feeling in you. In such a case, you won't mind that you are dreaming. You may enjoy it. However, much like a play, your daily waking dream doesn't only have roles that portray good people, only nice guys and beautiful, chocolate-flavored moments.

Actually, if all the parts in a play portrayed nice guys, then nobody would want to go to that play. It has to have some contrast or something dramatic: a love story with some heartbreak along the way, a villain, a death, danger and rescue. A life filled only with niceties is not enough to hold our attention, nor would it afford us the opportunity to grow.

We love the contrast. The experience of living and moving in the dynamic expression of life grants us that contrast. Can you imagine if you could only smile and laugh? It would be a horrible thing. Without sadness, how would you know what happiness is? Happiness would lose all sense of meaning.

In fact, we are completely addicted to the contrast and fun of experiencing. Something is attached to the thought of *what's next?*

But we tend to forget that all this is in the dream that we call our waking-state life. We have to wake up from even the sweetest dream—and we also have to wake up from the waking state and come into the space of pure seeing and being. This is our natural state.

The hypnosis of personhood within the dynamic aspect of consciousness can be likened to an actor who has identified with his part so strongly that he has forgotten he is an actor. Let's say you are playing a part in a Shakespearean play and you actually start to believe you are King Henry VIII. You forget that you are really Henry Brown. Your wife makes dinner, and when you don't like it, you throw it on the ground and shout, "Off with your head!"

And she just stares at you and says, "What is wrong with you? Who do you think you are?"

In much the same way, when we are identified with the sense of personhood, each of us plays a role. This role is not totally disconnected from Truth—it is also an expression of consciousness, but it is consciousness in a limited, contracted form. We have come to believe so deeply in the solidity of that person-identity that we cannot be who or what we *really* are—that is, the greater space of pure seeing and being in which the sense of the person appears. We look at our lives as if our standpoint were an objective reality—as if this is just the way it is. But the identity itself has never been an objective reality. It is deeply subjective. Like our dream walker on that beach, identity is a shape-shifter, always morphing into something else as it seeks to continue its dream life.

As you become ever more aware that you are the Self, the dream life—that is, the dynamic expression of life and the conditioned mind-set often associated with it—will come to have less signifi-cance. At a certain point, one finds sufficiency in just *being*. And whether the dream plays itself out one way or another, you're no longer swept away by every wave.

The dream is not real. The proof is that it does not affect everyone in the same way. The dream's effects depend upon the state and the capacity of the perceiver. If you know it to be a dream, its effects will be very weak. If you take it to be real, it will have a strong impact. So how long will the dream continue? That depends upon how quickly you wake up from the waking state.

As your discernment becomes more acute, you awaken to the recognition: Look at that—it's not real after all! I expended so much time and energy fighting this ghost, but now I see that it has never actually been real. Something inside would not let go of the attachment, of my *need* for the illusion to be real, which is why it kept *appearing* to be real. But now I see that I have always been free!

Beyond the 'I Am' Presence

If we just observe the workings of the egoic mind and don't invest any energy there, then the mind becomes quiet. When mind becomes quiet, only the natural sense of Being shines through. Everyone loves this shine, this natural way of being. It is called *amrit ananda*—*amrit* is the nectar of pure unassociated being, and *ananda* is the joy of tasting this nectar.

With this transition in orientation from person to presence, a shift occurs in the way one's life is experienced or perceived. This shift can be compared with the experience of someone returning home after a long period of travel. Everything is still there and familiar, but when people come and tell you the latest gossip, the effect it has on you is very different from before. You hear it, but none of it has any real impact upon you. It's as though your heart were cocooned in a space of peace, so that all such voices now seem very distant.

"Presence, what a beautiful place!" you may say. But for some people, even just the prospect of losing the context for their existence may frighten them to the core, and they may turn away from the Truth, thinking, *This isn't for me. I wouldn't know where I'd fit in anymore.* But this is just the voice of the egoic mind trying to disturb you.

As you come back into your Self and your attention remains focused in Self-awareness, you start to experience life with more detachment, and you take things a lot less personally. The things people say and think don't matter so much and don't affect you so deeply. You listen, but you don't listen with the mind. Rather, you find that listening simply happens energetically. Every now and then, something seems to get highlighted, and a response emerges naturally and spontaneously. It is not a state you're cultivating. Rather, this spontaneous power is expressing itself when you are presence.

All beings are happy in this state. However, some rare beings want to go beyond even the 'I am' presence. Why would anyone want to go beyond such a beautiful and harmonious state? Because, at the deepest level, even that state of presence is still not you. The presence is what the fragrance is to a flower. When you are in a position to witness this sense of presence, it too is seen as being phenomenal, and then you are immersed in the unspeakable—in the Absolute. You have become the flower, but, paradoxically, this flower nobody can find.

There is no sense of ownership here. You are in your purest state. You have no fight with life. You are not limited by race or religion—these don't touch you.

The rising of the moon and the movements of the planets, the passing of the seasons, and the ways of people—none of these things affect you. But you are not on another planet; you are right here.

You may be called a true human being, but you don't care whether that is perceived by others. You aren't busy determining what you will do. There's no need to speculate about the future, and you're not obsessed with the past. Night and day are no longer deep concepts for you. In fact, all concepts, even the great ones, have only a very limited impact on you.

The mind can still be used for everything, even for very ordinary things. It will still be there, but you will not venerate and obey the mind, which cannot function in its old role anymore. It turns over its service to the Supreme and acts only in goodness.

All of this is your kingdom. All of this is *you*. Once you become fully established in your own seeing, all is 'I am'—both the temporary aspect and the permanence that no one can see.

We can speak a lot about the movement from person to presence, but few words need be spoken about the shift from presence to the Absolute, for no efforts can reach it. Just enough will be said for you to understand that you are always in a position to recognize the true sense of Being.

Coming into the knowing of this Truth, moving from person to presence and finally to the Absolute, there is not a valve that closes behind you at each stage. Rather, now you know the totality. It is a bit like how, at one time, you had to put a lot of effort into learning the alphabet. But then you could write fluently, and you didn't have to look back and say, "The ABCs are all rubbish!" No, it is all there, still alive whenever you read or write. You know the alphabet and can teach it to your children, but you yourself have no need to study it anymore.

Similarly, as the Truth blossoms within your heart and waves of illumination wash through you, you will recognize the various stages and also the beauty of the totality—and you will move through life in that understanding.

That which Is is here already, but the shift of focus inherent in the changing over of power from person to presence will be tremendous. Presently we are focused on the objects of the mind—what we perceive in the outer world (in front of our eyes) and the inner world (behind the eyes)—in terms of thoughts, emotions, feelings, sensation, memory, desire, projection, judgment, and self-image. When these are believed to be real, they disturb the peacefulness of being; so the belief in their reality will have to go. But you will still be able to relate with other human beings on that level. The one who is awake is not a fool. The one who has moved into the realm of the Absolute is not dead; that one is fully alive and awakened from the waking state.

Just Sitting

In my hometown, there used to be a beautiful tree with black leaves, right there in the center of town. I've never seen leaves almost completely black anywhere else. One day I was walking by that tree and just felt that I wanted to stop and sit. Then, after about ten minutes, one friend came passing by:

"Hey, it's good to see you. So, just sitting watching the world go by, yeah?"

I said, "No, just sitting."

"Ah yes, deep in thought, eh?"

"No, just sitting."

"Ah, okay. So you're contemplating existence and all of that?"

I said, "No, just sitting."

"Ah, waiting for friends?"

"No, just sitting."

"Oh, I see that you want to be left alone."

I said, "No, just sitting."

How can you explain your Self? You don't know anything except that you are just here, immersed in this sense of presence. Sometimes the peace is so great, you cannot move. You cannot walk, and it feels like an effort to even open the eyelids. If you are in the company of people who think they know you, they will naturally want to know what's going on: "Why do you look like that? You're not looking so well!" Inside you're completely empty, yet you're full of peace and bliss. Still, they cannot see and may even worry: "Is there anything I can do?"

YOU ARE A NEWBORN TO YOUR SELF. TAKE A LITTLE TIME TO REST IN THE LAP OF GOD.

In that situation you may say, "I am fine. Actually, I'm very good." But the people around you still don't believe you. How to explain such things? It is best not to try. Just keep quiet and marinate in the fullness of this discovery. Know, verify, and confirm that even these blissful states are appearing in a vaster space of pure awareness.

If you are in this open space of Being, you may notice such special effects, but behind the appearances is immutable Being:

Being doesn't belong to any time frame.
Even in sleep, it experiences a sense of inner joy.
It has no story; it doesn't need a story.
It doesn't make plans; it doesn't announce,
"Next week I'm going to do this."
It is perfect, and perfection doesn't need a future.
It just keeps on manifesting unending miracles.
It is okay to feel overwhelmed by this bliss sometimes,
to stop and sit down or lean on a tree
because you are so full of joy.
It's not a problem that people may say, "Are you okay?"
What to do? What to say? You just stay as you are.

Give yourself a little time to grow in wisdom, to mature in understanding. Be firm in your conviction until you no longer even need conviction. Then you will be able to go anywhere and do anything without it leaving any footprints in consciousness.

You are a newborn to your Self. Take a little time to rest in the lap of God and to contemplate your Self. Marinate in your own Consciousness. Be with That as That.

It's one of the sweetest times you will ever have,
so don't miss it!
Not touching anything, neither going here nor there.
I want you to have the full taste of that immensity of Being,
of that silence unending,
of that joy inexhaustible.

Don't be in a hurry. Now is the time to stay put. Go home, zip yourself inside your sleeping bag, and don't come out until the sleeping bag kicks you out; just marinate in your Self. You don't need to learn more. You don't need more experience, more knowledge. It's not *more* that you need. That is only useful for people on a journey. You are not on a journey. You are always here, timelessly present.

Just sink into the ocean of Being.
Sit with this.

Use this life intelligently.
Be fully your Self.
Then your love can embrace the whole world,
and not just your family and friends.
You will no longer pick and choose,
and you will not judge.

The Truth is already inside you.
The personality is but a mask.
The Self alone is real.

May the seeds of pure understanding
come into full bloom within your Being.
So be it.

Om shanti shanti shanti

Glossary

Advaita Non-dual, not two. Also, the path of nondual teachings: everything is a part of and made of one non-dual consciousness. There is nothing outside of this oneness.

Bhakti The love felt by the spiritual seeker of Truth toward the Guru or God. The spiritual attitude of service to the Guru or God that helps purify the mind. The path of devotion and surrender, which is also known as bhakti yoga.

Brahman Supreme Being; the Absolute; the ultimate, nonphenomenal reality underlying and permeating all phenomena.

Chakras Energy centers of the vital force in the body.

Duality The play of interrelated opposites (e.g., you and me, pleasure and pain). Without it, no experiencing can take place. The world of names and forms in which we take ourselves to be individual entities relating with other individual entities.

Guru Literally, the dispeller of darkness and ego; an enlightened spiritual teacher or master who helps you dive within and realize the true Self.

Heart Not the physical heart or the emotional center; used as a synonym for the Supreme Self.

Jnana The path of knowledge, wisdom, and self-inquiry whereby one primarily uses the discerning power of consciousness (i.e., the heart-mind) to attain Self-realization.

Karma The law of cause and effect; action. As a spiritual path to Self-realization, it is also known as Karma Yoga, which emphasizes selfless action as a means to transcend the personal doer or ego.

Maya The divine illusion or dream of duality in the phenomenal universe.

Sri H. W. L. Poonja or Papaji (1910–1997) A disciple of Sri Ramana Maharshi, Papaji is Mooji's master. Although considered an Advaita Master, he is not confined to any particular tradition. His teachings emphasize that words can only point to ultimate Truth, but they never are ultimate Truth; one must directly realize the Truth through one's own investigation rather than relying on intellectual understanding.

Sri Nisargadatta Maharaj (1897–1981) A liberated sage of the nondual jnana path, known for his fierce demeanor and fiery wisdom as he ruthlessly and uncompromisingly points past the 'I am' consciousness straight to the Absolute.

Sri Ramakrishna Paramahamsa (1836–1886) A great Hindu saint and devotee of the Divine Mother Kali, as well as a fully liberated sage of the jnana path. In his indefinable devotion to God, he performed the practices of all world religions and confirms from his own direct experience that all religions lead to the realization of the same God-Self.

Sri Ramana Maharshi (1879–1950) A sage widely known for the power of his Self-realization, which he chiefly communicated through silence, as well as his devotion and union with the holy mountain of Arunachala in southern India. Sri Ramana recommends self-inquiry as an unsparing tool to erode the persistent habit of identifying with the ego. Mooji's own master, Papaji, is a direct disciple of Sri Ramana.

Sadhana Spiritual practice to transcend the ego, such as self-inquiry, meditation, reciting mantras, bhakti yoga, or jnana yoga.

Sangha A community of beings who, in following the call of the inner voice of Self-discovery, find themselves drawn toward a particular spiritual master who can guide them to realize the Truth.

Satsang Association with the highest Truth. Satsang also refers to meetings where seekers can ask questions and receive guidance from a teacher or master.

Vasanas Deep-rooted, habitual tendencies that belong to and reinforce a personal identity. They carry a strong emotional charge.

Yogini The sacred feminine force made incarnate; the goddesses of Hindu mythology, as well as the ordinary human woman who is enlightened, having both spiritual powers and deep insight into the Self.

Zen Emphasizes insight into Buddha nature and imparts that the potential to awaken is inherent in everyone. One awakens not by study or through rites and ceremonies, but by breaking through the boundaries of mundane logical thought.

Acknowledgments

INFINITE LOVE AND GRATITUDE to our master, Mooji Baba, for his unending love, support, wisdom, and guidance, not only for *Vaster Than Sky, Greater Than Space*, but also for showing us our true nature as timeless Awareness—the limitless Self.

We feel blessed and honored to participate in the sharing of our beloved master's pointings and are deeply grateful for the opportunity to be of service in this way. We would like to extend our gratitude to the Mooji Sangha and to all who supported this project in ways seen and unseen. Your presence and selfless service are the very evidence of the Truth that Mooji points us to.

Vaster Than Sky, Greater Than Space truly began at the hands of the transcribers, who spent many hours typing out the audio recordings word for word: Tania Gerich, Bill Spain, Clare Carney, Dominic Waithe, Jennifer Baquero, Kristina Hart, Lucinda Warner, Natalie Little Crow, Gayatri, Mantra, Niraja Mu, Shanti, and Sumantra. Once Abe Gutmann compiled the manuscript from satsang transcripts in consultation with Mooji, many more beings joined in to make *Vaster Than Sky, Greater Than Space* the book it is now. The Mooji Media Publications editorial team comprised Sumantra, Zenji, and Gayatri, with invaluable support from Jayani. Many thanks to those who offered feedback during the final stages: Nihal, Cyrus Irani, Laura Maria Palau, Mukti, and Sue McCormick. Special thanks to Amrita, who took the stunning photo on the cover, and to Sivaganga, who fine-tuned the various cover elements and images within the book alongside Mooji and the Sounds True design team.

At Sounds True we had the pleasure of working with the editorial, design, and production teams, which included Jennifer Brown, Jade Lascelles, Jennifer Miles, Beth Skelley, and Haven Iverson. Their talented off-site editor Joelle Hann in New York came on board right at the time she was already booked to attend the Silent Retreat with Mooji at Monte Sahaja in August 2015. Here we were able to meet face-to-face before commencing this vital part of the collaboration—a beautiful synchronicity!

Finally, we thank all readers whose love for Mooji and his teachings make this book necessary and possible. May your life be the evidence of Truth.

Om Shanti

About Mooji

ADVAITA ZEN MASTER MOOJI is unlike anyone else you are likely to meet. From the first encounter, his presence compels people to question their very nature and existence. His indefinable presence touches people from all walks of life, inspiring in them a natural sense of happiness and peace as they begin to discover who or what they truly are.

Mooji (Anthony Paul Moo-Young) was born in Jamaica on January 29, 1954. As a teenager he moved to Brixton, London, where he later worked as a street portrait artist and then as an art teacher in the local college. In 1987, an encounter with a Christian mystic inspired Mooji to "walk out of his life"—an expression he uses to convey the profundity of that meeting. In 1993, Mooji traveled to India, where seemingly by chance, he met his Master, Sri H. W. L. Poonja, or Papaji, as he is lovingly known by his devotees. At Papaji's feet, whatever still remained of an active ego in Mooji was finally uprooted. For several years following, he remained alone and fully immersed in his inmost being—the God-Self.

Some years later, recognizing Mooji's radiance, people began to approach him and simply sit silently in his presence. But there came a time when seekers started asking him about the nature of consciousness and the Self. These questions exploded inside his stillness and compelled him to go inward in prayer: "Father, you are bringing these people here. Now you yourself must answer them." Shortly after this, the power to guide these seekers directly arose spontaneously inside Mooji's heart. He could see from inside the Being the answers to their questions—not in words, but in spirit. From this emptiness, guidance would simply manifest, and it continues so to this day.

Mooji's presence exudes a loving compassion and devotion, and his unity with Truth is potently shared through self-inquiry—the unsparing light of nondual wisdom that dispels the delusions and suffering common to human experiencing. Each one who meets Mooji with a genuine urge for pure understanding, for freedom, is pulled by the profundity of his unconditional love and the power of his pointings into the recognition of the infinite Self we already are.

Mooji continues to share satsang worldwide with all who are attracted by his light and yearn to discover their true nature.

Further Information

FOR INFORMATION ABOUT Mooji's work and schedule please visit:

    Mooji.org

For information about Mooji's other books: *The Mala of God*, *White Fire*, *Before I Am*, *Breath of the Absolute*, and *Writing on Water*, and for satsang recordings in audio and video format, please visit:

    Mooji.org/shop

For online video and audio recordings of satsang with Mooji, please visit:

    Mooji.tv

Mooji is also on Facebook: Facebook.com/moojiji
    and on YouTube: Youtube.com/moojiji

About Sounds True

Sounds True is a multimedia publisher whose mission is to inspire and support personal transformation and spiritual awakening. Founded in 1985 and located in Boulder, Colorado, we work with many of the leading spiritual teachers, thinkers, healers, and visionary artists of our time. We strive with every title to preserve the essential "living wisdom" of the author or artist. It is our goal to create products that not only provide information to a reader or listener, but that also embody the quality of a wisdom transmission.

For those seeking genuine transformation, Sounds True is your trusted partner. At SoundsTrue.com you will find a wealth of free resources to support your journey, including exclusive weekly audio interviews, free downloads, interactive learning tools, and other special savings on all our titles.

To learn more, please visit SoundsTrue.com/freegifts or call us toll-free at 800.333.9185.